THE ASPIRING HIKER'S GUIDE 1
MOUNTAIN TREKS IN ALBERTA

BY GERRY SHEA, DC

RMB
Victoria Vancouver Calgary

Rocky Mountain Books
#108 – 17665 66A Avenue
Surrey, BC V3S 2A7
www.rmbooks.com

Rocky Mountain Books
PO Box 468
Custer, WA
98240-0468

Library and Archives Canada Cataloguing in Publication

Shea, Gerry
    Mountain treks in Alberta / Gerry Shea.

(The aspiring hiker's guide ; 1)
    Includes bibliographical references and index.
ISBN 978-1-897522-79-0

    1. Trails—Rocky Mountains, Canadian (B.C. and Alta.)—Guidebooks. 2. Hiking—Rocky Mountains, Canadian (B.C. and Alta.)—Guidebooks. 3. Trails—Rocky Mountains, Canadian (B.C. and Alta.)—History. 4. National parks and reserves—Rocky Mountains, Canadian (B.C. and Alta.)—Guidebooks. 5. Rocky Mountains, Canadian (B.C. and Alta.)—Guidebooks. I. Title. II. Series: Aspiring hiker's guide 1

GV199.44.C22A45856 2010   796.51097123'32   C2009-907201-7

Front cover photo: Stunning sights while hiking the Mosquito Creek trail
Back cover photo: Southwest view of Lake Minnewanka from its northern shoreline
All photos by the author unless otherwise stated.

Printed in Canada

Rocky Mountain Books acknowledges the financial support for its publishing program from the Government of Canada through the Book Publishing Industry Development Program (BPIDP), Canada Council for the Arts, and the province of British Columbia through the British Columbia Arts Council and the Book Publishing Tax Credit.

This book has been printed with FSC-certified, acid-free papers, processed chlorine free and printed with vegetable based inks.

Mixed Sources
Cert no. SW-COC-001271
© 1996 FSC
FSC

Disclaimer
The actions described in this book may be considered inherently dangerous activities. Individuals undertake these activities at their own risk. The information put forth in this guide has been collected from a variety of sources and is not guaranteed to be completely accurate or reliable. Many conditions and some information may change owing to weather and numerous other factors beyond the control of the authors and publishers. Individual climbers and/or hikers must determine the risks, use their own judgment, and take full responsibility for their actions. Do not depend on any information found in this book for your own personal safety. Your safety depends on your own good judgment based on your skills, education and experience.
    It is up to the users of this guidebook to acquire the necessary skills for safe experiences and to exercise caution in potentially hazardous areas. The authors and publishers of this guide accept no responsibility for your actions or the results that occur from another's actions, choices or judgments. If you have any doubt as to your safety or your ability to attempt anything described in this guidebook, do not attempt it.

Contents

Easy backpacking trails can be appealing to family members. The author was accompanied by his son, and his son's girlfriend, into the Mosquito Creek campground. Candace Ostertag on the Mosquito Creek Trail.

Chapter 1
Backpacking Equipment

Purchasing backpacking equipment is an important investment, so time, effort and care should be used to make quality decisions. The choices should not be as simple as going to a big-box store and buying the cheapest gear available. In fact, the standard rule is that the lighter the equipment is, the more expensive it becomes. Cost and quality make the difference between an efficient, lightweight, comfortable backpacking trip, and a heavy, tedious, backbreaking, painful one.

Backpacks

When shopping for a backpack, speak with a qualified person in a reputable outfitting store, and set aside considerable time for fitting. Each person is unique, and a proper fit is vital for successful trekking.

Backpacks are categorized as either internal frame or external frame design.

Internal frame
The advantages of the internal frame backpack include its body-hugging capability and its lower centre of gravity. Both of these help to produce superior balance. Freer movement of arms and less bounce are other conveniences as well. The internal frame pack also has less tendency to get hung up on tree branches and overhangs. The disadvantages are a modest tradeoff: although the lower centre of gravity creates better balance, it will place more stress on the shoulder harnesses, while the snugger body fit will generate perspiration on the wearer's back. However, an air mesh frame will help to counteract the effects of excessive perspiration, as it permits air circulation between the pack and the wearer's back. This air circulation is no longer an exclusive feature of external frame backpacks.

External frame

The external frame backpack is less popular because of its awkward manoeuvrability. It does allow for larger loads, though, with the ability to lash objects onto the frame with greater ease, making it easier to load and unload. It also lets air circulate between you and your pack, although this gap compromises balance. The external frame backpack produces a higher centre of gravity, resulting in a more erect body posture.

Very seldom are external frame packs seen on the trail today, and therefore the remainder of this discussion will involve only internal frame backpacks. Internal frame packs are loaded from either the top (top loaders) or the side (panel loaders). More advanced backpacks have the convenience of both top and side access.

Top loaders

This has now become the standard, most common type of backpack. The best argument for a top loader is the easy loading capability, as their basic design is a tube shape with a drawstring on top. This design is great for stuffing gear into, because the pack expands outward as gear is stuffed into it from the top. Additionally, the top loader has no zippers in critical pressure areas, so these packs can withstand excessive overloading, whereas the panel loader must be zipped up after it has been loaded.

Panel loaders

Panel loaders are outfitted with a huge, u-shaped, zippered opening on the back of the pack. The benefit of this design is easy access to articles near the bottom without having to unpack the entire load. The problems with this style are that panel loaders cannot be packed as densely as top loaders, and that the zipper is under constant pressure when the pack is fully loaded and rupturing can occur.

Additional features

Other extras to look for in a backpack are simple items such as side pockets, external lash straps for securing bulky items to the outside, and compression straps to stabilize the load. A divider inside a backpack is an additional benefit, as it allows for easier access inside and less stress on the base of the pack. A divider usually separates the lower third of the pack from the upper two thirds, and limits the tendency for everything to pile up at the bottom.

Fitting a backpack

Torso length, not overall body height, is the measuring guide for fitting a pack. Fitting should be worked out in the standing position with the feet shoulder-width apart to allow the effect of gravity to give a more accurate reading. In this stance, measure the distance from the first thoracic vertebra (the prominent one where the neck meets the upper back) down to the sacral base (just below the bottom vertebra in the low back). This distance will provide the torso length. Smaller than 45 cm indicates a small pack, while 45–50 cm is considered a medium size. Larger than 50 cm is a large backpack.

After determining the approximate size, throw the pack on your back. It should be stuffed with a few camping articles to add some weight and bulk, expanding the pack to its packed size and providing a somewhat real-life simulation. The pack should be adjusted so that the weight is distributed to the hips and shoulders equally. The hip belt should rest below the waist at the hips. Make sure that the load-lift straps can be accessed by reaching behind your ears. A sternum strap is important, as it assists in determining the forward and backward centre of gravity, but its position on your sternum should be decided by comfort. Most sternum straps can be raised or lowered to allow for maximum comfort.

Clothing

The three fundamentals required for a successful trip are dryness, warmth and comfort. Although warmth and dryness go hand in hand, comfort is similarly important. With the ever-changing weather in mountain regions, these three crucial requirements are necessary to maintain a happy, enthused outing.

Undergarments and shirts

Given that the perspiration created from a hike can create as much moisture in clothing as a torrential downpour, it is essential to purchase the appropriate clothing for both inevitabilities. Although cotton and wool may be comfortable, they have a tendency to absorb moisture and broadcast it throughout the rest of the garment. Consequently, when they become wet they will remain wet for some time. That is why a water-resistant, wickable fabric is preferable.

Wickable fabric is chemically treated 100 per cent non-cotton polyester, which is designed to expel moisture. It works on the principle of removing moisture from the skin and dispersing it into the atmosphere instead of absorbing it. It does the same with externally applied moisture. At least three different companies produce wickable material, but Patagonia's "capilene" is by far the best performer.

When it is near the end of the day and the sun goes down, the temperature can drop significantly within minutes, and a wet cotton shirt can bring on chills and clamminess, greatly increasing the chances of hypothermia. With wickable material, however, dryness is usually achieved by the time the tent is set up, making for a more comfortable night.

To get the maximum benefit from wickable material, it should be worn in layers. The skin layer pushes moisture out to the external layer and from there out into the atmosphere. Another wonderful feature of this fabric is that it is so tightly woven that it resists the sun and the bugs but still allows skin to breathe.

An alternative to wickable material is a polyester and nylon thread, as it will still repel rainwater better than cotton. An application of a water-resistant chemical product such as Nik Wax TX Direct will create a water-resistant, wax-like coating on the material. This solution is mixed in the washing machine with the polyester shirt and run through a normal wash cycle. It is not waterproof, but it resists water quite well.

Outerwear

Over top of shirts, the next layer of material should be a jacket, preferably fleece. Fleece comes in a variety of thicknesses and qualities. Although this retains warmth and moderate amounts of dryness, it will trap moisture from the inside as it is repelled from the skin. Therefore, recognizing when to remove the fleece is important, as it should be a warming layer only and not used during a strenuous part of a hike. Fleece is warm, lightweight and reasonably compressible.

The other practical choice for an outer layer is down-filled clothing. Although down is light, compressible and warm, once wet it becomes heavy, bulky and cold. Even if caught in a light summer shower it soon becomes a burden.

Pants

Absolutely never wear blue jeans for hiking, as they are far too heavy and bulky, they absorb water and the material is extremely thick, creating excessive amounts of perspiration. Jeans do not have an elastic waistband, and not even a belt will keep them up when wearing a backpack. As well, they cause chafing of the sensitive skin of the inner thigh and groin. When jeans get wet, they also become heavier, and take days to dry out.

Synthetic material is the best choice for hiking, as polyester and nylon are much lighter and more compressible for packing than cotton. Synthetics are also warm and have the ability to repel water. Once more, wickable material is an excellent choice for pants as well.

During the heat of the day, when short pants can be worn, the same materials should be used, again avoiding cotton. Wearing shorts in a light shower keeps you cool, saves the hassle of donning rain pants and reduces the chances of getting your long pants wet, which may be needed later in the evening.

Raingear

Raingear is a critical component of any hike, and even on cloudless, hot days, a thunderhead could be lurking behind the next mountain. A light mountain drizzle can be quite nice, but a day-long downpour is not very uplifting. Being prepared for a cloudburst will make or break a successful summit.

There are only two materials and two styles of raingear to choose from. Let's look first at the materials.

Gore-Tex is the best rain material yet invented, but because it is the best, it is also the most expensive. Other manufacturers have tried to duplicate it, to no avail. Gore-Tex works on a similar principle as capilene, as it pulls the moisture from underlying material and expels it as vapour through tiny pores in the fabric. The great advantage of this system is that only vapour can sneak out through these tiny pores, and for that reason only vapour can sneak back in. Rain droplets cannot get through. Thus, when body temperature rises, the resultant heat converts the perspiration into vapour, which escapes through the Gore-Tex micro-pores and into the stratosphere, allowing underlying clothing to remain dry, even in the rain.

The other material used in raingear is pure polyurethane backing with a 100 per cent nylon face. There are some variants, such as polyvinyl chloride (pvc) and polyester, but they all ultimately have the same properties. They perform exceptionally well to keep the water out, but they don't breathe from the inside outward. Perspiration gets trapped inside the jacket, creating a moist environment. To counteract this, some models come with zippered armpit and chest vents to compensate for the inadequate ventilation. The greatest payoff for the polyurethane and nylon fabric is that it is about one-fifth the price of Gore-Tex.

As for the two styles of raingear, the differences are glaringly obvious. The poncho style should only be used for day hikes when shelter is close by. The poncho is too ineffective, as well as awkward and bulky, making even simple hand operations or removing a pack rather tedious. The other glaring drawback is the gaping hole at the bottom, exposing the lower body to the elements. The lower limbs become wet from water splashing up from the ground and from runoff from the poncho itself, allowing precious body heat to be lost. Never depend on a poncho raincoat when scrambling. At high altitudes, the loss of heat combined with damp clothing could rapidly lead to extreme hypothermia.

The pant and jacket style retains heat very well, and if secured at the wrists and ankles properly one should be comfortably sealed from the elements. The jacket and pant style allows much freer movement, keeps moisture out and retains body heat.

Gloves

Gloves are a piece of equipment that may seem unnecessary when packing on a glorious hot day, but even on a bright, blue summer day, subzero temperatures are common on a mountain summit. A mixture of wool, Lycra and spandex materials is very versatile, creating a fabric that is warm and elastic. Ideal for the outdoors, these gloves are lightweight and fold up into a little ball for packing. A waterproof treatment for these gloves is also available. Lightweight glove liners made of Thinsulate or comparable material are a viable alternative. Again, these are lightweight and compressible and can be stuffed anywhere in the pack.

Boots and socks

Comfort and support are particularly important when looking for the proper boot. Do not buy a large fit with the intent of wearing layers of socks for warmth, as warmth is the responsibility of the footwear. A large-fitting boot will produce blisters and foot cramps and cannot be broken in properly. Conversely, a tight fit will impede blood flow and create cramps in the feet.

It is important to spend some time with a knowledgeable outfitter to get the appropriate help with this vital purchase. Tell your salesperson what the boots' primary function will be, the type of terrain you expect and the distances you plan to go. It is necessary as a backpacker and a scrambler to buy good-quality footwear. There are many different types of leather and synthetics to choose from, so it is vital that you sample footwear until you find the right pair for you. You do not want them to let you down in bad weather and rough terrain.

High-cut fabric or leather boots with an inner membrane of Gore-Tex or Sympatex offer good support and most importantly can be waterproofed. One-piece leather boots present superior support and have the best waterproofing capabilities, since they have fewer seams. They are very durable, and leather has natural moisture-wicking capabilities.

With either of these designs, a wickable inner lining such as Cambrelle is advisable, to absorb perspiration, which is then pushed up and out through the leather or Gore-Tex membrane. Some boots are made with a leather lining for comfort, but the leather absorbs the moisture and holds it longer than Cambrelle, making the inside of the boot wet and mushy.

Most boots will require additional waterproofing. This should be done long before the first hike, permitting ample time for the product to be absorbed into the boot. Either the spray-on petroleum type or the type that is rubbed into the material will help maintain dry and warm feet.

Proper socks are also important, and there are several combinations to choose from, including a mixture of acrylic, wool, nylon, spandex or polypropylene, worsted wool and stretch nylon. Some manufacturers use cotton mixed with Hollofil. The decision depends on two main factors: an individual's level of perspiration and their tolerance of synthetic materials. If you have significant tolerance of synthetic material, then a wickable material is recommended to keep moisture away from feet. Alternatively, try wool socks, as they are somewhat wickable. Never use cotton socks, however, as they readily absorb moisture. When cotton socks get wet, they slide around inside your boots, creating hot spots on the heels and pads of the feet. Another suggestion is to use wickable liners inside of socks. These push the moisture from your feet into the sock almost immediately, keeping the feet free of perspiration moisture.

Sleeping bags

Sleeping bags are categorized by fill, shell, size, shape, internal space, weight, compatibility and temperature rating.

The required temperature rating depends on the time of year that the bag will be used, the elevation and the local climate and environment. Be aware that the weather in the Rockies can change overnight, and it is not uncommon to encounter temperatures below freezing combined with snow even in July and August. Therefore, a bag that is suitable for subzero temperatures should be considered, even if it is intended for summer use.

Of the several types of fill, down is the best choice. The rest are all synthetic imitations of down. The superb features of down are that it has high loft (the higher the loft, the warmer you will be), it is lightweight and has great compressibility. The only drawback is that when it gets wet it becomes useless. It will no longer keep you warm, it loses its loft and gets heavy and it takes forever to dry. You might as well pull up the tent and head home.

The synthetics are a decent, less costly alternative to down, and of course, some are better than others. The main advantage of synthetics over down is that when they get wet, they will dry out in a reasonable time, allowing the journey to continue. They do not have the loft or the compressibility that down has, and synthetics are slightly heavier. Hollofil, Hollofil 2 and Quallofil, though considered a technological alternative to down, are the least-regarded synthetic fills. These bags are bulky, heavy and do not compress well, but are inexpensive. Primaloft, Primaloft 2, Liteloft, Microloft and Thermolite Extreme are better performers but still they are not the best. Although they are quite compressible, they will not stand up very well in the long run. Polarguard, Polarguard 3D and Polarguard HV are the top synthetic fills and currently hold 75 per cent of the market. They are very compressible, have good loft, which they maintain longer than the others do, and they are very durable. They are also lighter than the other synthetic fills.

When purchasing a sleeping bag, fit it to size as well. There are only three adult sizes: small, medium and large. The bag should leave room to pull the hood around your head while leaving a few inches at the bottom for leg movement, but not too much legroom. All empty space in the bag must be warmed with body heat, and wasted space means wasted heat. Spending the night warming up dead space in the bottom of a bag can lead to a long, cold night. Consequently, a mummy bag is far superior for retaining warmth than a regular rectangle bag. A common problem with some campers, however, is the claustrophobic sensation in a mummy bag, so if you have difficulty in elevators, you will probably have trouble in a mummy bag. To respond to this problem, some mummy bags are outfitted with elastic waist and leg bands to allow for expansion. Another pertinent feature is a double-ended zipper (a zipper pull at both the top and the bottom of the bag), as this allows partial unzipping along the bottom of the bag to permit cooling and movement. There are good rectangular bags available for those who just cannot tolerate a mummy bag.

Sleeping pads

The purpose of a sleeping pad is to supply comfort and insulation from the cold ground. Without one of these, the smooth, soft ground will soon feel like cold, hard concrete.

Of the three types of sleeping pads, the self-inflating kind is preferable, as it offers greater cushioned comfort and good insulation. They are light, compact and easily compressed to fit into a backpack. A minor downside with self-inflating pads is that they can puncture, but they are easily re-paired and are usually equipped with a repair kit. Self-inflating pads come in either a full body length size or a three-quarter body length model for less weight and bulk. These single-chambered, self-inflating air mattresses become one-half to three-quarters of an inch thick when fully blown up. The term self-inflator is used because the mattress will inflate of its own accord when unpacked and rolled out with the valves open. Some lung work is still required to attain maximum loft. A more recent addition to the self-inflation family is the down-filled mat. These dramatically reduce heat loss and compress smaller, as most down products do, but they are a nuisance to inflate. Down becomes lumpy and ineffective when moist, so the pad must be inflated with a bellows. The down mat design consists of ribbed chambers with baffles to prevent the migration of down, as well as allowing a higher loft. The design and materials provide superior comfort and warmth, but at a price four to five times that of a standard self-inflator. A variation on this product is the non-down, ribbed self-inflator. This chambered, baffled mattress supplies loft and comfort without the warmth of down, while still giving greater warmth than the standard models.

The other main category of sleeping pad is the closed-cell type, which does not cushion as well as the self-inflating pads but offers better insula-tion for a comparable thickness. These are somewhat bulky, though, and do not compress at all, so they must be rolled up and strapped to the outside of the pack. The only advantage of closed-cell pads is that they are far less expensive than the self-inflating ones.

Lastly, "blue foam" pads are very cheap, but are often of little use. To sleep comfortably on the ground, you need a sleeping pad with enough loft to keep you comfortable and warm. Blue foam is just not dense enough or thick enough.

Tents

The two most important factors to consider when purchasing a tent are weight and quality. The remaining features such as ventilation, materials, quality and ease of setup will fall into place correspondingly. Choosing a tent is really quite uncomplicated, but a tent should nevertheless be purchased at a backpacking retailer rather than a department store. Department stores and warehouse depots generally do not carry the quality of tent required for backpacking.

The style of tent, whether dome or tunnel, is an individual taste, as is the size. Style and size ultimately determine the weight, so decide whether the tent is going to be used by a single hiker or a group. Once the group size has been determined, the choice of style is fairly easy. A dome should be used for a group of three or more, while the tunnel type is generally for a single hiker or a pair.

Poles are a key component of the tent. Aluminum and tempered aluminum poles are superior to fibreglass, as they are stronger, more flexible and lighter. They are, of course, more expensive. Even so, the choice is usually made for you, as the higher-end tents will come equipped with aluminum, shock-corded poles.

The material of the tent is also a consideration. A three-season tent, made of lightweight nylon fabric, is sufficient for late spring, summer and early fall backpacking and is the most common type. For camping in winter, a mountaineering tent, four-season tent or even a convertible tent is advisable. These are made of nylon and polyester, making them heavier.

Speed and ease of setting up a tent are especially important in the dark or in adverse weather. There are three basic designs for attaching a tent to its poles: clip style, pole sleeves or the grommet system, though the simple grommet system is rarely used anymore. Colour-coded clips with matching-colour pole ends are possibly the easiest method for erecting a tent.

Proper ventilation is another concern when looking at tents. On a hot summer night with a barrage of insects, ventilation becomes essential. Double doors with no-see-um mesh are a godsend, as cool air is allowed to flow without opening a flap and letting the bugs in. Some versions also have a mesh ceiling to support stargazing.

Even if the manufacturer insists their tent is waterproof, it still needs to be seam-sealed. This is a straightforward procedure requiring little effort but a bit of time. Set the tent up in an open area such as a backyard, and roll or brush the sealant on every stitch, seam and zipper in the tent. Do the same to the fly tarp. Use a seam sealer that is recommended by the tent manufacturer.

A footprint is a tent accessory that is particularly valuable, and is simply a second floor that goes under the floor of the tent. They are not a standard component, but are add-ons that are usually hard to find and costly. It is far easier and cheaper to purchase thin nylon from a fabric outlet and have it sewn by a local tailor. The footprint should be slightly larger than the floor of the tent, with grommets installed where the tent pole ends are situated. A footprint increases the longevity of the tent floor as well as keeping it dry.

Cookware

It seems that with any backpacking equipment there is always a trade-off between weight and quality, and cookware is no exception. With four types of material to choose from, the decision becomes a personal preference. Aluminum, stainless steel, non-stick coated aluminum, and titanium are the choices.

Heat dispersion on the bottom of the pot depends on the thickness and type of metal. Thicker is definitely better for heat distribution, but of course it is heavier. Aluminum has one-third the density of stainless steel, so when using aluminum the result will be a thicker pot with less weight. Aluminum is also a better conductor of heat than stainless steel, even if the stainless steel is thicker.

So why consider the stainless steel? Stainless steel is stronger and does not dent or scorch nearly as easily as aluminum. Accordingly, stainless will last longer and is easier to clean than aluminum.

The third material, titanium, is incredibly light, extremely strong and effortless to clean. The downside is its susceptibility to scorching, and if the meal is not constantly stirred, the bottom of the pot will burn and so will dinner. Titanium is also incredibly expensive.

Non-stick aluminum is the best all-round choice. Its density is comparable to the relative thickness of steel, and therefore the heat is dispersed evenly. It is stronger than basic aluminum cookware and it is by far the easiest to clean. However, non-stick coated aluminum is two to three times the cost of the stainless steel and is somewhat heavier.

Backcountry stoves

There are two types of backcountry stoves to choose from: those that use canister fuel and those that use liquid fuel.

The canister type comes in a variety of styles, and all of them contain a blend of pressurized fuel. The fuel is either butane or a mixture of butane and propane. Regardless of the fuel mixture, all canisters are pressurized. Of the two types of canister stoves, the blended fuel type produces a hotter flame. Even so, all fuel canisters will fade in cold weather and at high altitudes.

Almost all liquid fuel stove systems use inexpensive white gas, which burns more efficiently than either type of canister fuel. The liquid fuel stove is also more efficient at high altitudes and cold temperatures. What's more, when a liquid fuel stove runs out of gas, it only requires refilling the empty cylinder, whereas with canister fuel the entire canister has to be replaced.

The canister stove may burn somewhat more powerfully than the liquid fuel stove at first, but it loses its efficiency proportionately as the pressure and fuel both decrease. With a number of canister units there is no effective way of controlling the fuel output. Liquid gas stoves come equipped with a pump and a flow control valve, allowing far greater regulation of the fuel. The Mountain Science Research (MSR) "Pocket Rocket," however, is an extremely lightweight, ready-to-use canister system that does permit control of fuel flow.

The only real benefit of the pressurized canister system is the easy setup and use. By attaching the canister to the stove unit, it is ready to be lit and it heats up immediately. The liquid gas method is more finicky and time-consuming to set up. But even with liquid gas stoves there are levels of craftsmanship, and MSR's Whisperlite International has been proven as a reliable stove for decades. It boils water quickly and simmers very effectively even in high winds, rain and cold and at high altitudes.

Water containers

The types of water containers are different for backpacking and scrambling, but with either activity, attaching the canister to the outside of the pack is preferable for easy access. For backpacking, a single 1-litre container is adequate, as streams and lakes are encountered frequently along the trail. At least two 1-litre containers should be carried while scrambling, though, since water is not readily available.

In fact, on a scramble, when clean water is found, it is prudent to rehydrate immediately and replenish your water bottles, because there usually is no water on the sides of mountains or their summits. It is a common error to rely on what may be shown on a map or remembering that there was water up this mountain last year. Always take advantage of any water you come across, without depending on what may lie ahead, as more often than not there will be no water whatsoever on a mountain scramble. Go with the intent of taking with you all the water you'll need.

Conversely, a backpacking route will almost always have plenty of water along its course, and if not, the campgrounds are always situated near a clean water source. Hydration is imperative to avoid muscle cramping, lightheadedness, fainting and heatstroke.

Additional equipment

Items that are necessary for a successful backpack trip but do not require detailed descriptions are items such as:

bug spray
bear spray
sunscreen
extra clips and straps
short length of rope
all-purpose tool
flashlight
toilet paper
matches
bandana
hiking pole(s)
water filter system
toque

Red Squirrel along the Mosquito Creek Trail.

Chapter 2
Backcountry Management

Most beginner backpackers do not know what to expect at a campground after a day of hiking, and this can be somewhat unnerving. Without the knowledge of where to camp, cook, store food, get water, urinate, dispose of waste or brush your teeth, a backcountry blunder is inevitable. This sort of difficulty may not be important to a handful of backpackers, but the backcountry campground requires a community effort if it is to remain pristine, and many hikers take this on with vigour.

Campsite location

Selecting a campsite is relatively easy in the Canadian Rockies backcountry, as the campgrounds in the national parks are designated areas, and random camping is rarely permitted. Sites are easily located in the campgrounds, since some are marked, some have tables and some even have wood shavings to set your tent on, but all of them are at least trampled down.

The first consideration in deciding on a campsite is proximity to water. Almost all campgrounds are along streams or lakes. The decision depends partly on the weather. A good general rule is to stay 50–75 m away from water on cooler days, since the temperature may be as much as 10 degrees cooler beside the water. On hot days, camping a little closer to water is preferable. Naturally, the water should also be conveniently accessible for repeatedly refilling your containers.

Level ground is also of primary importance. Sleeping on well-planed, flush earth is not always possible at campgrounds, but the more level the ground is, the more peaceful the night will be. Even with no-slip sleeping pads there is still a tendency to skid down the pad if camped on a slope. If there is no choice, and there is only sloped ground available, be certain to sleep with your head higher than your feet to avoid awakening with a pounding headache.

Explore the region for insect life as well. Anthills, beehives and stagnant water (mosquitoes) should be passed by. Insect-infested trees not only present the obvious insect problem, but the affected tree may be structurally weakened as well. Additionally, look for rodent dens, game trails and porcupines in trees.

Ideally, a campsite with trees to shelter your tent from the wind is preferred. Nevertheless, these surrounding trees must be examined for potential danger. Campsites with dead or diseased trees or branches, as well as trees that have fallen and are leaning on others should be bypassed for a safer area. A stand of trees is one of the safest places to be during a lightning storm, but camping under a single tall tree is dangerous because lightning will go for the single tallest object in an area.

If the campground's dining area is communal, do not set up too close to it. Not all campers clean up after themselves and animals quite often do this for them. Since some campsites are equipped with rustic picnic tables, you may find yourself cooking and eating close to your tent, so be absolutely sure that no scraps have been left behind.

Proximity to the outhouse is also a consideration. Although there are typically not any tent sites next to outhouses, some are closer than others. There is no bedside light to switch on, and stumbling through the dark, bumping into tents and trees, is painful and embarrassing. Campers that urinate beside their tents are endangering all other backpackers in the campground because the odour attracts bears and rodents.

Tent set-up

After selecting a tent pad, the next step is to erect the tent. The tent should be set up soon after arrival, as the weather can change quickly and darkness can arrive sooner than anticipated. It may be tempting to have a drink or lunch first, but the tent should go up before too long, leaving the exploring and playing until later. The tent is your only shelter from the elements for a few days, and if it is not ready before an unsuspected cloudburst arrives, then sleeping bags, clothes and equipment become drenched and the trip is ruined.

If the camp is somewhat organized before leaving for some day hiking, then one can at least get warm and dry if the good weather does not hold. After the tent is up, the sleeping pads, bags and clothing should be tossed inside immediately – again, to keep them dry in the event of rain. Next, the food, cooking utensils and all other odorous belongings should be pulled up the bear poles. Backpacks, now empty of food, should be placed under the tent vestibule. Bears and rodents are enticed by almost any smell, so when your food is placed up the bear pole, your soap, bug spray, sunscreen, toothpaste, stove, pots and anything else emitting a scent should all go up with it.

Consider setting up the tent with the door facing south so the morning sun can shine in to warm the tent up. Wind direction should be noted if the bugs are bad or if it is a hot evening. Tents with twin doors should be oriented so as to allow the breeze to circulate through.

Cooking/eating area

In the backcountry, where you eat is just as important as what you eat. Some campgrounds have common areas where everyone cooks and eats, while others have a table at each campsite. Communal areas are designed to keep food and odours away from tents, and they should be used when provided. These areas are usually central and well marked with signage or a structure. If they are not marked, search for obvious signs of use, like rocks or logs in a circle or signs of cooking. Cook and eat at these areas until the meal is finished so that food is not spread throughout the campground.

Estimating the quantity of food to cook is tricky but essential, as there is no garburator or wastecan and all of the food cooked must be consumed. Food waste cannot be tossed into the outhouse, because this attracts rodents, and it certainly cannot be thrown into the streams or lakes. All campgrounds have a designated grey-water disposal area, but it is intended for wastewater that may contain only a few scraps, not for throwing out leftovers. The only other alternative is to contain the waste in a plastic bag or container and consume it later or pack it out. After eating, all morsels of food, paper, matches and plastic must be picked up from the ground or table. Every last scrap.

Food should not be consumed near the tent, and eating in the tent is absolutely discouraged, including gum and candy. Bears are attracted to the scent of food, and if anything has been chewed in the tent, a bear's nose will lead him there. Not only will the food odours be absorbed into the tent fabric, but cooking in the tent could run the risk of carbon monoxide poisoning.

Washing your dishes

Cleaning up utensils, dishes and pots in the backcountry is a bit of an art, and an attempt should be made to use as little water and soap as possible. Heating water in the cooking pot you've just used not only detaches stuck food but also provides hot water for cleaning the other items. A bit of biodegradable liquid camp soap on a reusable cloth works well to remove particles from dishes and utensils. The soap, water and waste should be dumped into the grey-water site. Rinse with a bit of clean water and wipe dry.

Washing yourself

Hygiene in the woods is necessary but not difficult. Before cooking any meal or making a hot beverage, use some of the boiled water to wash with. Do not wait until after the meal when the pot is grimy or after you have done the dishes and must boil more water, as this only wastes valuable fuel. Pour the hot water onto a clean cloth and apply a dab of camp soap, then wash body parts with this soaped cloth. Pour hot water onto another clean cloth and use for rinsing. Wring these clothes out into the grey water area and hang them to dry.

Brushing teeth is just as easy, and odourless toothpaste with organic ingredients can be purchased at most health food stores. A small amount of water with a modest amount of toothpaste is all that is required. Brush and then spit again into the grey water pit. Please do not wash your body or brush your teeth in the lakes or streams. If everyone uses one small designated grey-water area, then waste and pollution are not spread all over the countryside.

Outhouses

Just a few words on outhouse use. We all know what should be done in there, but some of us tend to overuse this facility. The only waste that goes in, other than the obvious, is toilet paper. No food, garbage, cans or plastic should be thrown down this hole. These items must be used or packed out. Skunks and porcupines are attracted to such smells, and can really ruin the campground's atmosphere.

Maintaining the campground

The minimalist rule for campground maintenance is to try to leave the campsite in better shape than you found it. Stay on the established trails leading to the water source, bear poles and outhouse. Trampling on delicate flora can eradicate them quickly, as these plants only have a short time to grow and reproduce. If they are destroyed during this short window, they cannot reproduce the following year.

The same principle applies to digging drainage trenches, uprooting rocks, picking flowers and snapping branches off trees. The campground should be left as close to its natural state as possible.

Looking southeast on return from Dolomite Pass.

Chapter 3
Scrambling

Fitness

To climb mountains and venture into the backcountry, strong legs and lungs are equally important. Many factors determine an individual's level of fitness needed to accomplish the goals set out in this guide. Even though one does not require an athlete's physique, it is still important to tone up muscles and work the heart and lungs long before the season arrives. You cannot decide in June that it is time to get in shape for a hike in July. It just will not work.

It is understood that everyone is a unique individual and we are all different, so each and every one of us will have distinctive expectations, and our discipline will not be the same either. However, you get out what you put in, and it is much easier to scramble up a mountain while being in trim condition with heart and lungs that are strong than being flabby and gasping for air. Every pound lost in the winter and spring is a pound less that must be carried up a mountain or into the bush. Every extra kilometre logged on a treadmill is rewarded with less effort in the summer.

There are three basic components to physical fitness: muscle strength, muscle flexibility and cardiovascular strength. There are numerous ways to increase your heart health and exercise your lungs. Walking, swimming and cycling are great. Stair climbers, jogging and low impact aerobics are also superb ways to gain wind and endurance. If you live in a snowy climate, snowshoeing and cross-country skiing are activities that will improve circulation and strengthen your legs. The best method to prepare for the scrambling season is to walk up mountains or hills that may be in your area.

Muscle strength and flexibility are just as significant as the cardiovascular system, and there are just as many ways to work on this. All of the previously mentioned activities will boost leg power, but will not improve the suppleness of these muscles. Basic stretching exercises can be found throughout the Internet or in libraries, but for something a bit more intense try yoga.

For the most part, everyone will work at their own pace and with the equipment at their disposal. It should be rather simple to enter into a plan for the off-season, but try a bit of variety to ease the boredom. If it becomes increasingly difficult to develop a fitness program, consult a professional. Discuss your goals and comfort level and get started.

Scrambling equipment

Scrambling equipment is essentially the same as backpacking equipment, with only a few changes. The pack and footwear will be different, and some notable additions must be highlighted.

Day pack

The features to look for in a scrambling pack are similar to those of a full backpack, but the pack is smaller. The main difference between the two activities is that scrambling is more physically intense and therefore creates excessive amounts of perspiration. A moderate backpack trip may take three to five hours, whereas an easy scramble will take five to eight hours. A scramble of 1000 m of elevation gain is, of course, only 1 km in distance, but for the most part, it is uphill and will take the better part of a day. That same distance while backpacking should take no longer than 15–30 minutes. With these key elements to consider, weight, air mesh frame and padding become vital.

The area of most perspiration will be the region of most contact, and this area is where the pack contacts the back of the torso. Perspiration cannot escape if there is a simple nylon pack frame resting on the spine. An air mesh frame will absorb moisture and even repel it in some cases. Ideally, an elevated mesh, which outlines contact areas, not only absorbs moisture but also reduces the amount of friction between pack frame and body.

Additionally, with the tremendous physical work of scrambling, it becomes apparent that you should pack as little weight as you can possibly get away with. Purchasing a small pack in itself reduces weight, but it also cuts down on the extra, non-essential gear that will be carried along. Daypack sizes vary greatly, but a scrambling pack should be in the range of 20–35 litres capacity.

Hip belts and shoulder straps that are padded and adjustable are optional features that should be considered. This allows far greater comfort, permitting transference of the pack weight from shoulders to hips and vice versa. A sternum strap is another necessary item, as it pulls the load forward when cinched, easing the natural tendency of the pack to pull the load backward. These small features may not seem important now, but it is a tremendous relief during an all-day climb when the load can be rearranged ever so slightly.

A lid that allows you to shift and elevate the top load is another feature that makes for a less strenuous hike, as it shifts the weight and the centre of gravity. A proper lid will be capable of carrying several frequently used items, like bug spray and sunscreen.

Ideally, the scrambler's daypack should have external straps for fastening items that require immediate access such as an ice axe or helmet.

Footwear

Although hiking boots are suitable for scrambling, a lighter "approach" shoe is recommended. These shoes are especially suited for scree slopes and rock hopping. Due to their lighter weight, there is generally less fatigue on the legs, feet and ankles. Approach shoes are generally constructed of synthetic materials, so there is the risk of getting wet feet. Good approach shoes will have a ring of rubber around the entire shoe, including the toe, flanks and heels, as these areas are susceptible to damage from scraping on rocks while climbing. Good grip is essential, more for descending than ascending, and a cushioned insole is also advisable. As with good hiking boots, a backpacking outfitter will have the best selection and quality. Try on several pairs until you find the right one.

Additional equipment

Many items that are necessary for a successful backpack trip are also essential for a scramble. However, a few other items are recommended for a scramble:

bug spray
bear spray
sunscreen
extra clips and straps
short length of rope
all-purpose tool
flashlight
toilet paper
matches
bandana
hiking pole
water filter system
toque
ice axe (only required for high elevations)
helmet
emergency foil blanket

Leaving the forest behind and entering the vast meadows toward Dolomite Pass. The magnificent Dolomite Peak is in full view.

Chapter 4
First Aid

A first aid kit should contain all components necessary to treat everything from mosquito bites to fractured legs and gaping wounds. As frightening as it may seem, if an accident occurs there will be no help, and even if you have cell phone service, assistance is still hours away. It is therefore essential to be prepared to care for yourselves. Many backcountry first aid kits not only hold all of the essential tools but also come with instructions for treating emergency injuries. Take a kit along on all trips.

Since blisters and hypothermia are the most prevalent ailments suffered while trekking, they will be the only ones discussed here.

The most common ailment in the woods is blisters, and they can occur on all areas of the feet as well as ankles. The best way to treat a blister is to avoid getting one at all, and knowing how blisters occur will help prevent them. Blistering results from friction, and friction between material (socks and boots) and your skin creates a shearing stress on the skin. This shearing action causes separation of the outer, supple layer of skin that covers the deeper, more secure layers. As the bones in your foot move one way and the boot moves another, the skin is trapped between the two and rubs on the sock material, creating a hot spot. Due to this constantly repeating friction, the outer layer of skin at this spot becomes separated from the tougher inner layers, and the area of the separation gradually fills with lymphatic fluid, creating the blister.

Treating a blister before it becomes a full-blown mess is imperative in prevention. At the first sign of a potential problem, stop walking and attend to the problem immediately. Many great trips have been ruined by deciding to limp the last one or two kilometres to the campground. Treating a hot spot is easy, but before administering any treatment, wash and dry the afflicted area first. Then apply an antibiotic ointment over the region, finally covering the blister with moleskin or Spenco 2nd Skin.

For a fully developed blister, the treatment is only slightly different. Again, clean and dry the affected section before proceeding with the treatment, as an infection can easily occur if the area is not kept clean. After this, the bubble must be broken with a clean needle to release the fluid. Disinfect the needle with an antiseptic wipe, puncture the blister, and release as much of the fluid as possible by applying pressure with clean hands. After the screaming subsides spread an antibiotic ointment over the blister and cover with moleskin or Spenco 2nd Skin. This should be repeated two or three times per day in the same manner and washed and dried with fresh ointment and moleskin applied.

Hypothermia is another common syndrome easily acquired but easily avoided, and being prepared is the best prevention for this malady. Even on the clearest, sunniest day in the mountains, the weather will change without notice. While standing at the base of a mountain on a hot day it is hard to believe that the temperature at the summit can be below freezing, but quite often this is the case. Dress accordingly for the heat, but make certain you've packed cold-weather apparel too. Gloves, toques, jackets and an emergency blanket are indispensable articles to take when either backpacking or scrambling.

Lake Minnewanka from the shoreline trail.

Chapter 5
Backpacking Trips

1. TONQUIN VALLEY, AMETHYST LAKES CAMPGROUND

The walk to the Amethyst Lakes and campground is unlike any other. The route of this wonderful trail begins with a pleasant stroll through a forest, then meets up with a raging river, which it travels alongside. The trail then crosses an avalanche slope, and on the other side it climbs upward beside the avalanche path for about 400 m. At the zenith of the rise, the track opens up to a spectacular rambling plateau presenting unequalled views of lakes, ranges, peaks, streams and glaciers. The final destination provides tranquility, peace, exploration and history.

DIFFICULTY ▲ ▲ ▲ ▲ ▲
DISTANCE: 20 KM
ELEVATION GAIN: 351 M

Trailhead: GPS: N52 42 09.3 W118 03 35.9
                                Elevation: 1743 m

Summit of switchbacks: GPS: N52 40 43.3 W118 11 34.7
                                Elevation: 2094 m

Amethyst Lakes Campground: GPS: N52 41 44.1 W118 15 09.5
                                Elevation: 1980 m

Trailhead: Travelling south from Jasper on the Icefields Parkway, turn right onto Highway 93A. Take Highway 93A south for 5.2 km until you reach the Edith Cavell Road. Climb the Edith Cavell for 12.5 km and park at the Tonquin Valley Trailhead.

Within a few short minutes, the trail crosses a bridge and encounters the first fork in the trail. A well-marked sign directs you to stay right. Soon a slow, gradual descent into the Astoria River Valley begins. Once

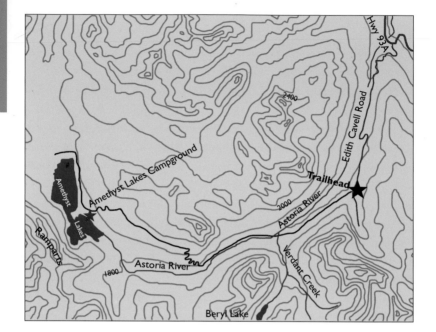

in the valley bottom the trail parallels this river for two to three hours while periodically crossing feeder streams of the Astoria River, including Verdant Creek at kilometre 4.3. You will cross the churning, blue-grey Astoria itself 4.6 km into the hike. Aside from the incredible beauty, the first notable landmark that is encountered is the Astoria Campground at 6.8 km, taking somewhere between 1.25 and 1.5 hours to get to. This campground is removed from the main trail, giving campers a little privacy from the throngs of hikers that have been known to come here. The campground is quite small, with only six to eight sites and a privy. Bear poles are also provided.

Continue for an additional 20–30 minutes until you reach a fork in the trail. A trail sign at this point marks the Tonquin Valley Trail to the right, while the left fork crosses the Astoria River and goes to Chrome Lake, Outpost Lake and the Emerite Valley. The left route will take you to Amethyst Lakes via the Wates-Gibson Hut, but it's a significantly longer choice. The main trail makes its way through a horse gate and corral to resume the Tonquin Valley Trail. Within 10–15 minutes from the horse gate is a massive avalanche slope of resistive quartzite. Notice the jagged edges of this stone, as opposed to the smoother edges of limestone avalanche rock. These edges remain so sharp because resistive quartzite, unlike other rock, is not weathered away by rain, snow or wind, but only by frost heaves.

After passing below this massive slope the trail begins the arduous yet inspiring upward climb of switchbacks that come in and out of the forest as they run upward alongside the avalanche slope. The switchback section rises to 2194 m (about 400 m elevation gain). Roughly an hour later the trail levels off, opening up to low-growth trees and exposing an amazing view of the Ramparts. The Ramparts are a series of peaks at the headwaters of the Fraser River, with Parapet Peak on the south end of the ridge as the highest point. These stunning, unmistakable landmarks tower over the western shore of Amethyst Lakes, creating one of the most startling backdrops in the Rocky Mountains. The British Columbia/Alberta boundary runs the length of the Ramparts, bisecting them down the middle.

The upper valley trail consists of long, undulating hills which are remarkably fun to hike. The stunning scenery up in this openness makes the climb up the switchbacks easily forgettable. Along the upper trail, kilometre 12.9 marks the junction to Switchbacks Campground, while 3.5 km later (16.4 km total) you will intersect the junction to Clitheroe and Surprise Point campgrounds. From here you will descend back into the forest as the trail takes you downhill to Amethyst Lakes Campground.

History

This valley hike is full of history that did not occur here. The name "Tonquin" was assigned by the Geographic Board of Canada to pay homage to the ship of the same name, which was commissioned by John Jacob Astor in 1810 to establish a permanent trading post at the mouth of the Columbia River. During a trading mission on Vancouver Island, the crew of the Tonquin were killed by Indians agitated by the insulting behaviour of the ship's captain, Jonathan Thorn. The Astoria River is named after

43

John Jacob Astor, while Franchère Peak, in this vicinity, is derived from one of the only few survivors of the massacre.

The Tonquin Amethyst Lakes Lodge was constructed on the shores of Amethyst Lake (actually two connected lakes) by Fred Brewster in 1939 and is still in operation today. Along with the campground and a Parks cabin, the lodge is the central charm on the shores of the Amethyst Lakes. The lodge, campground and Parks cabin are located at the narrows joining the two lakes, while another lodge is settled at the north lake.

On one of my last trips into the valley, in 2006, I was fortunate enough to encounter a hiker coming out of the Tonquin Amethyst Lakes Lodge where he had just enjoyed the weekend. With this elderly gentleman hiker were his daughter and son-in-law and their young children. As luck would have it, he stopped for a breather at the same spot where we were resting. He was alone at first, in the lead, with the rest of the family having trouble keeping up with his pace. He was 70 years old, and the weekend had been to celebrate the 50th anniversary of his time as a youth working at the lodge. He had worked summers packing food in to the lodge, fetching water and cutting firewood, and in his spare time he climbed the surrounding mountains. The one thing that still sticks in my mind is that he said that nothing had changed except that the trees had grown taller. Other than that, the lodge, lake, mountains and streams were just as he had left them 50 years before.

View of The Ramparts with Amethyst Lakes in the foreground from the upper valley trail. Tonquin Valley trail.

Throne Peak from the upper valley trail of the Tonquin Valley trail.

One of several streams on their journey to the Amethyst Lakes.

The South Jasper Range. One of many amazing sites along the Tonquin Valley trek.

45

2. GLACIER LAKE CAMPGROUND

Incredible beauty at the beginning and at the end, a gorgeous streamside walk and an elevating walk in a park-like forest describe this trail. There are few campgrounds in the Rockies that can be characterized by one single feature, and Glacier Lake Campground is one of them. The sight across the lake, with looming peaks to the far westerly edge, is worth planting yourself on the beach to focus on this one single vision of lake and mountain. Exploring the far reaches of the west end of the lake is a day trip that sees only modest traffic. Discovered in the spring of 1807 by David Thompson, the lake was named by Dr. James Hector of the Palliser Expedition 51 years later.

DIFFICULTY ▲ ▲ ▲
DISTANCE: 8.9 KM
ELEVATION GAIN: 189 M

Trailhead:	GPS: N51 58 23.9 W116 45 34.5
	Elevation: 1446 m
Summit of trail:	GPS: N51 56 18.3 W116 49 14.8
	Elevation: 1622 m
Glacier Lake Campground:	GPS: N51 55 38.6 W116 50 14.1
	Elevation: 1433 m

Trailhead: Drive north on the Icefields Parkway for 78 km from its junction with the Trans-Canada Highway, or 1 km north of Saskatchewan Crossing. The trailhead parking lot is on the west side of the Parkway.

The trail begins innocuously enough, planting you in the midst of a classic Rocky Mountain forest of lodgepole pine and spruce trees. At the 1 km mark, as the trail crosses the North Saskatchewan River, the forest suddenly opens to display an instant view of the Howse River Valley and its surrounding peaks. This is quite a staggering sight when it is not expected. Another 1.4 km places the trail at the Howse

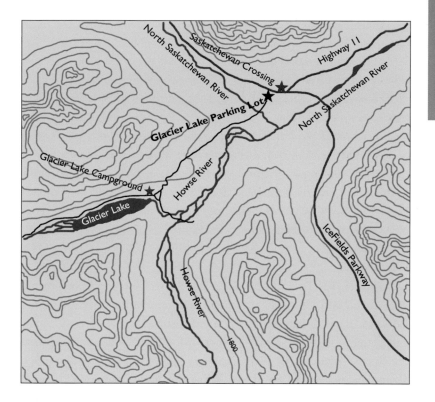

River lookout. A host of peaks awaits your viewing, including Mount Murchison to the far left, Mount Erasmus to the near right and Mount Outram straight ahead.

Travelling down to this valley bottom places the trail on the north side of the Howse River for about 1.5 km. The walk alongside this glacial silt river is exhilarating, as the vistas of the surrounding peaks become captivating. Sadly, though, within 20–25 minutes the trail leaves the Howse to pursue a lesser tributary and re-enters the narrower views within the forest. In the mountains, what goes down must go up, and the trail begins to ascend to 1622 m. After levelling off, the path roams through the lovely forest for 20 minutes before dropping sharply down to 1433 m to Glacier Lake Campground. The sharp descent is occupied by exposed roots and rocks, making it somewhat treacherous.

47

The decline ends just before the lake, and the trail forks with signage directing hikers to the campground. It is almost impossible to make your way to the campground without checking out the beach first, since the sight of the lake and surrounding peaks draws you like a magnet.

The day trip will take you around the north end of Glacier Lake to the far west end. The lake is 3.8 km long and 750 m across, making it the fourth largest lake in Banff Park. A coarse trail parallels the water's edge to the end of the lake where it becomes less visible as it reaches the flats of the braided glacial runoff stream feeding Glacier Lake. Continue to follow the main branch of the Glacier River for 4–5 km farther to approach Southeast Lyell Glacier. Climbing moraines on the right side of the river offers even more amazing views of the glacier.

History

Although Howse Pass was recognized as a pass by David Thompson in 1807, the braided Howse River was first explored in the early summer of 1806 by a scout dispatched by Thompson named Jacques Finlay. Finlay and his crew of three departed Rocky Mountain House and followed the North Saskatchewan River until they met up with a tributary which Thompson later named the Howse River after Joseph Howse, a Hudson's Bay Co. explorer who had crossed the pass in 1809. Having cut a crude trail through the pass, Finlay returned to Thompson with map in hand.

The following year, 1807, David Thompson made a successful crossing and established a trade route with Interior Natives. This choice would have been a possible CPR route with established hotels had it not been for a minor encounter Thompson had with an angry Chief Big Bear on a return trip in 1810. Big Bear had just been defeated in battle by rival Indians with the help of firearms from white traders. With Big Bear camped just upstream, Thompson decided to avoid conflict and left the area, subsequently discovering the much longer Athabasca Pass. Big Bear and his Peigan tribe closed Howse Pass to any further trade, and for the next 50 years Athabasca Pass was the primary route for fur traders, leaving the Howse to the Peigan. In 1858 James Hector sought out the Howse, and in doing so discovered and named Glacier Lake.

Glacier Lake.

Howse River Valley from Viewpoint.

49

3. FRYATT VALLEY, BRUSSELS CAMPGROUND

Although this is a relatively long hike, it has a comfortable degree of elevation gain. There is only 445 m difference from the trailhead to the campground. In fact the first 11.6 km is a flat meander through an uncluttered forest of lodgepole pine with scarcely any change in elevation. The Upper Fryatt Valley is a short 5-km day hike from Brussels Campground and is an exquisite land of pools, streams, vanishing rivers, tarns, meadows, glaciers, snow, subalpine forests and waterfalls that encourage showering. There is so much to see here and yet it is compressed into a short, tidy hanging valley. This hike may not the longest in this guide, but it presents a true remote backcountry experience.

DIFFICULTY ▲ ▲ ▲ ▲
DISTANCE: 17.2 KM
ELEVATION GAIN: 445 M

Trailhead:	GPS: N52 38 55.2 W117 53 59.0
	Elevation: 1215 m
Brussels Campground:	GPS: N52 30 39.8 W117 52 30.2
	Elevation: 1660 m

Trailhead: Drive south on Highway 93 (Icefields Parkway) for 32 km from Jasper to the Athabasca Falls turnoff. After turning right onto Highway 93A, continue for 1.2 km to the Geraldine Lakes road. Another 2.1 km and this gravel road will arrive at the trailhead for Fryatt Valley.

Leaving the Geraldine Lakes parking lot, follow a trail into an open forest of pine skirting the west shore of the Athabasca River. This delightful walk wanders for 11.6 km until reaching the inconsequential Lower Fryatt campground. Parks Canada allows the use of bicycles for this first stretch, because of the length of the trail and the lack of elevation change. Before arriving at the Lower Fryatt campground, the trail crosses the Geraldine Lakes outlet stream at kilometre 2 and a mound of glacial till overlooking the Athabasca River at kilometre 8. Glacial till is a heterogeneous mixture

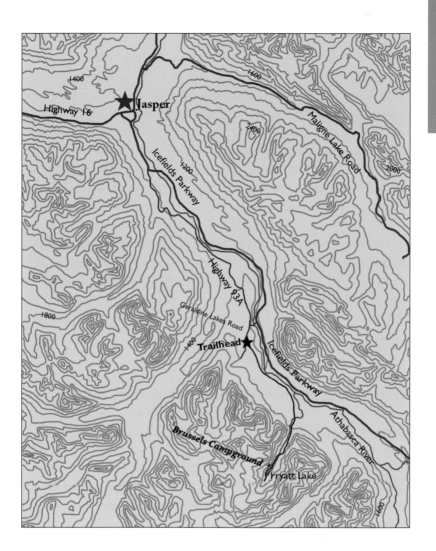

of clay, sand, gravel or boulder-size particles deposited beneath and within glacial ice. Looking southeast from here you'll see a magnificent panorama of Mounts Christie and Brussels.

After crossing Fryatt Creek at Lower Fryatt Campground the path now begins to climb somewhat steeply upward through an increasingly thinner forest of subalpine growth. The grade ascends for 4.2 km acquiring

325 m before finally diminishing at the Fryatt Creek Bridge at kilometre 15.8. At this point, the wonder of this place on earth begins to unfold as the first sights of the Fryatt Valley begin to appear. The vast openness of the valley upon exiting the confines of the forest is unexpected yet welcome. Stick to the trail by following cairns and well-placed rocks in the stream to reach Brussels Campground 1.3 km up the valley.

Exploring this valley as well as the Upper Fryatt eliminates any hesitation about making this long voyage. Leaving the campground, climb over a small alluvial fan and descend slightly to reach Fryatt Lake. This is a beautiful place to just sit and relax. Spaces like this are rare and not usually encountered in our daily lives. Take as much time as needed here; all you have here is time and beauty. Just beyond the lake is a limestone rock wall called the Headwall. Fryatt Creek falls over the headwall to feed Fryatt Lake. To explore the Upper Fryatt Valley, climb the excruciatingly steep headwall, gaining 200 m in less than a kilometre. At the top of the headwall the upper valley opens up as you hike past the Alpine Club of Canada's Sydney Vallance Hut.

History

Fryatt valley, creek and mountain were named after Captain Charles Algernon Fryatt (1872–1916) by the Alberta-British Columbia Boundary Commission. Brussels Campground and nearby Brussels Peak take their names from the Great Eastern Railway steamer *Brussels*, which was under Captain Fryatt's command. The *Brussels* was an unarmed merchant ship that made regular runs on the Rotterdam/British East Coast route during the First World War and was very successful in eluding the Germans.

On two occasions, March 3 and March 28, 1915, Captain Fryatt avoided attack by German u-boats. In the latter incident, he was able to attempt to ram the submarine as it surfaced to line up a torpedo on the *Brussels*. The u-boat was forced to dive, narrowly averting a collision. Captain Fryatt reported, "You could have easily hung your hat on the periscope as she lay alongside us." Fryatt was awarded a gold watch for each of his encounters with the submarines.

However, 15 months later, on June 23, 1916, his luck ran out as he was surrounded and captured by a convoy of German torpedo boats. In Bruges, Belgium, on July 27, 1916, Captain Fryatt was tried, found guilty of being a franc-tireur, or unlawful combatant, and executed later that evening, having written a farewell letter to his wife and six children.

As the trail emerges into the Fryatt Valley, the sky opens to offer many sights. This is one of many peaks that line the northern flank of the valley.

The Athabasca River seen from a mound of glacial till on the Fryatt Valley trail.

4. SKOKI COUNTRY, HIDDEN LAKE CAMPGROUND

This campground is the gateway to the Skoki backcountry area. Skoki Lodge is an ideal day trip from Hidden Lake Campground, but since the lodge is 7.3 km beyond the campground, it's a longer day hike though still quite attainable. More than half of the hike takes place on a gravel service road, and more than half of the elevation is achieved before heading into the wilderness, making the short backwoods portion of the journey utterly enjoyable.

DIFFICULTY ▲ ▲ ▲ ▲
DISTANCE: 7.2 KM
ELEVATION GAIN: 499 M

| Trailhead: | GPS: N51 28.535 W116 05.984 |
| | Elevation: 1695 m |

| Hidden Lake Campground: | GPS: N51 28 32.1 W116 05 59.1 |
| | Elevation: 2194 m |

Trailhead: Leaving the village of Lake Louise, head north over the Highway 1 overpass up Whitehorn Road. Turn right onto Fish Creek Road at 1.7 km and then continue for an additional 1 km until you reach the parking lot.

The marked trailhead begins at the Fish Creek parking lot and begins a gradual climb almost immediately up the Temple access road. The first 3.9 km of the trail is a gravel road leading to the Lake Louise ski area. Although trudging up this road feels far removed from the backcountry experience, it really is not, as the road runs through dense forest and over rushing streams. There is a lot of work involved in gaining 320 m of height on this stretch, but the mind can be taken away from the struggle as the road follows the delightful Corral Creek and its feeder streams. The gravel road ends at the Lake Louise ski hill parking lot. Look for the "Skoki Valley Trail" signs off to the right and pick it up going up a short, steep incline.

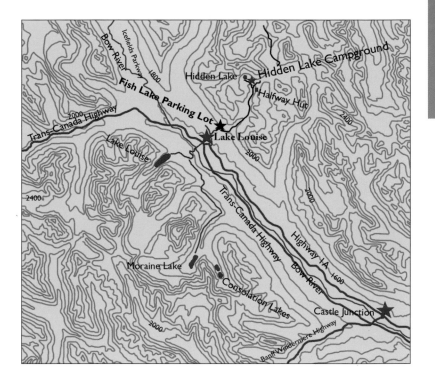

After travelling 2.4 km through a subalpine forest alongside Corral Creek, you'll find the forest becoming sparse and then finally opening into a meadow. There is only 900 m remaining to the campground, so take your time in this openness. Stop, look, listen and smell. Tourists have been passing through this same spot for at least 76 years; the history can be felt here. As the trail approaches the campsite, the history can also be seen as the Halfway Hut comes into view on the right at 7.1 km. There is well-marked signage showing the way to the hut and the campground to the left. The hut was used mainly in the winter as a stopover for guests on the way to Skoki Lodge. Standing outside the door of the Halfway Hut looking southwest, enjoy the view of the looming, snowcapped peak of Mount Temple.

Going back to the main trail, carry on up to the Hidden Lake campground junction and turn in to the campground. It is not situated on the lake as the name suggests, but the lake can be explored 1.2 km north of the campground. This typical Rocky Mountain tarn lies beneath Pika Peak and Mount Richardson, both of which are within 1.2 km of the lake but appear much closer. The trail of this short hike to Hidden Lake is surrounded by beautiful wildflowers. If a day hike to Skoki Lodge is too overwhelming, Boulder Pass (Ptarmigan Lake), Deception Pass and Baker Lake are all easily accessible, at another 1.5, 3.9 and 6.1 km respectively. At kilometre 10.5 on the Skoki Valley Trail (3.4 from Hidden Lake Campground) is the signed junction for Baker Lake to the right and Deception Pass to the left. Either trail leads to Skoki Lodge, but the Deception Pass route is the quickest, with 3.9 km to travel from the junction.

History

This campground is the gateway to the Skoki backcountry area. Skoki Lodge was constructed as a ski resort in 1930, with the first guests arriving in the spring of 1931. It was the first one of its kind in western Canada. The lodge was built for Cyril Paris and Cliff White by Earl Spencer, and their structure is still fully operational today, welcoming guests throughout the summer and winter seasons.

Although he was certainly not the first explorer in the area, James Porter named the region during a 1911 journey. The name was originally spelled "Skokie" in his notes, but that was eventually assimilated to Skoki over the passing years. Porter took the name for the region from a Potawatomi Illinois Indian tribe word meaning "swamp" or "bog." He also took the liberty of naming many other natural features nearby, including the Wall of Jericho, Protection Mountain, Merlin Castle, Tilted Mountain, Skoki Mountain and two lakes: Douglas and Redoubt.

The Halfway Hut in the Hidden Lake region was built as a resting place, shelter from storms and an overnight stay for tourists bound for Skoki Lodge. It's a spartan facility, yet a haven of warmth and comfort for many travellers caught in a winter's storm. After perishing in an avalanche while skiing in 1933, a lodge guest from Boston, Massachusetts, was said to have haunted the Halfway Hut for many years afterward. Dr. Raymond Edwin Allen Christopher Paley set out from the lodge to ski unaccompanied after lunch on April 7. He departed without notice and proceeded up the side of Fossil Mountain, which had been deemed extremely unsafe just that same day. As he neared the top of the slope an avalanche slab gave way, taking Dr. Paley with it. No one knows what prompted his action, apart from Paley himself. Sadly, he was only 25 years old.

Plenty of exhilarating excursions lie beyond the Hidden Lake Campground, such as a day trip into Boulder Pass.

The wide-open approach to Hidden Lake Campground is stunning.

5. CASCADE RIVER FIRE ROAD TRAIL, CASCADE RIVER BRIDGE CAMPGROUND

This fabulous outing is the gateway to the wilderness of the Cascade Valley and the remote east corridor of Banff National Park. This vast section of the park is less travelled by hikers because backpacking trips into the heart of this region are quite lengthy, the trails are often not maintained and grizzly bears frequent the area. Beyond Cascade River Bridge Campground, bridges are not always operational, making fording streams necessary at times.

DIFFICULTY ▲ ▲
DISTANCE: 6.5 KM
ELEVATION GAIN: 79 M

Trailhead:	GPS: N51 14 32.4 W115 30 42.0
	Elevation: 1468 m
Cascade River Campground:	GPS: N51 17 15.2 W115 32 02.3
	Elevation: 1547 m

Trailhead: At the east entrance into Banff Township get onto the Lake Minnewanka Road. Take this road for 6.5 km to the Upper Bankhead Picnic Area parking lot. A sign marks the trailhead at the east end of the parking lot.

This gentle hike travels through groves of balsam poplar and forests of subalpine fir. Slow-moving streams, marshes and beaver-dammed ponds are the features of this wide fire road trail. The trail commences as a narrow single track trail through a small field of yellow buttercups. This quickly enters a forest of subalpine fir, which soon evolves into a double-track fire road.

This fire road remained active until 1984, when two of the main bridges collapsed, and in 1988 the parks service banned the use of motorized vehicles on all fire roads in the park. They then decided to narrow the bridges on this trail to pedestrian width and open it up to foot and bike traffic. When the fire road was constructed in the 1930s it cut deep into the

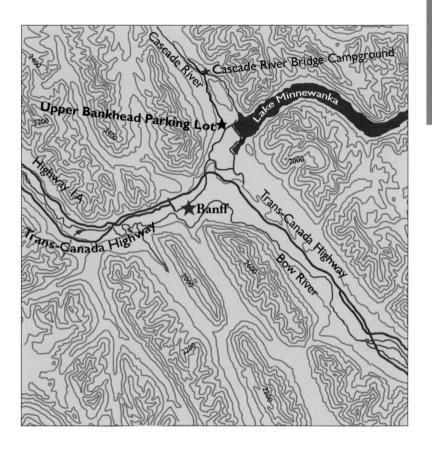

remote wilderness, and it is now the departure point of an enormous trail system extending into an immense region.

At 500 m, the distinct scent of packhorse and mule stables is unmistakable. From the stables the trail ascends modestly for about 100 m, plateaus and then descends into a grove of balsam poplar and spear grass. From this grove of deciduous trees the trail climbs gradually for about 1–1.5 km, then levels off into a coniferous forest once again.

The advantage of walking this fire road is the wide-open feeling which extends the view of the Palliser Range to the north and east (directly ahead and to the right) and Cascade Mountain to the west (left). The road also permits groups to walk side by side. For the remaining 4 km, the trail meets with wetlands of streams, ponds and marshes on either side of the road. Wetland grass varieties of horsetail, spike moss and sedge are in abundance throughout this area, with pond-lilies and duckweed being common in these ponds. Bottom-feeding ducks, shovellers and widgeons can be observed here early in the summer and again later into September to October. Yellow warblers, common yellowthroats, American redstarts and red-winged blackbirds spend time around these marshes as well.

The road ultimately drops down to the Cascade River, Cascade Bridge and the campground, which is a fully equipped backcountry campground containing tent pads, rough table and chairs and an outhouse.

History

Cascade mountain and river take their names from the waterfall at the southeast end of the mountain. "Mountain where the water falls" comes from the Native word "minihapa." James Hector abbreviated the meaning, and in 1858 he named it on August 15 and climbed it on August 16, even though he did not reach the summit. The summit was not achieved until 1887, by L.B. Stewart and Tom Wilson. In 1911 Cascade River and Valley obtained their official names from the mountain of the same name.

6. GERALDINE LAKES CAMPGROUND

The Geraldine Lakes trail should only be travelled during dry, sunny conditions. The trail is lost on the route around the second lake in a maze of large boulders covered with crust lichens, making the hike extremely slimy and slippery. Even without the lichens, large rounded rocks are dicey on their own when wet. Although there are four lakes in the chain, the third and fourth ones are without a trail and require a tremendous amount of work to access.

The trek to the campground presents two wonderful waterfalls, two lakes and a pond, forest, scree and two gruelling climbs. A day well spent.

DIFFICULTY ▲ ▲ ▲ ▲ ▲
DISTANCE: 6.2 KM
ELEVATION GAIN: 400 M

Trailhead:	GPS: N52 37 42.0 W117 54 51.8
	Elevation: 1496 m
Geraldine Lake #1:	GPS: N52 36 54.1 W117 55 50.6
	Elevation: 1613 m
Top of First Waterfall:	Elevation: 1694 m
Geraldine Lake #2:	GPS: N52 35 30.6 W117 56 23.8
	Elevation: 1896 m
Geraldine Lakes Campground:	GPS: N52 35 17.8 W117 56 42.0
	Elevation: 1896 m

Trailhead: At 32 km south of the junction of Highway 16 and the Icefields Parkway is the turnoff for Athabasca Falls, which is also the south end of Highway 93A. Take this road on the west side of the parkway and drive past the Athabasca Falls parking lot for 700 m. On the left side of Highway 93A is the Geraldine Lakes Fire Road, also the

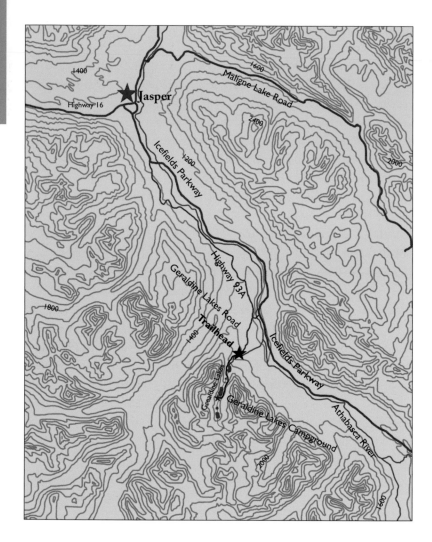

entrance for the Fryatt Valley trailhead. Drive the fire road for 5.6 km, to the end of it.

The first 1.8 km takes you through a dense forest of evergreens which climbs gradually for 117 m before it reaches the first of the Geraldine Lakes. The trail sticks close to the west shoreline, creating damp feet and frustration during high water, so try to veer slightly inland to stay dry. At the end of the first lake the path fades, becoming less and less conspicuous as the journey continues. From here on in, follow yellow markers and cairns and the bits and pieces of trail as it materializes.

Here at the end of the first lake is the first of two wonderful waterfalls encountered on this hike. Stay to the right and clamber up the side of the falls for 81 m, reaching a short valley. There is a second lake here, but it is not *the* second lake. Follow cairns and trail to the left side of this pond before walking alongside it through the trees. At the far left reach, the path scrambles up what feels like a perpendicular wall for another 202 m. This is a test for boot traction, as there is nothing to grasp and the hillside is loose pebbles and scree.

While creeping your way toward the next level you will undoubtedly stop to rest lungs and legs. Enjoy the moment by turning around and glancing north. Sit down and take a break; take as long as you want to take it all in.

On top of the waterfall the second lake comes into full view. There is much rock hopping and the trail is sparse. Stay low, avoiding the trails to the viewpoint up the right bank at the near end of the lake. The way to the campground is on the left (west) shoreline. The route is mainly rocks and boulders with some bits of trail through bush. As much as rock hopping is fun, it is dangerous. There is more than a kilometre of this to the campground at the distal inlet stream, so fatigue is also a consideration while playing on the rocks. The campground is primitive, with four or five pads, a bear pole and a privy.

Day hiking from this point is obvious but dangerous. There is no trail to the third and fourth lakes, and minor navigational skills may be required.

History

It seems hard to believe that with all the early exploration going on all around the Geraldine Lakes chain, it was not until the 1930s that someone set foot in this remarkable series of hanging valleys. Athabasca Pass and Whirlpool Campground are a measly 5 km over the next northern range, and the Fryatt Valley is only 8 km south of the lakes over Mount Fryatt.

The outlet stream from the Geraldine Lakes entering the Athabasca River is so close to the Whirlpool and the Fryatt that it is difficult to understand how all of this was ignored or not found.

Regardless, the valley was first entered by Frank Wells sometime during his tenure as park warden for the Sunwapta district. He was given the position in 1924 and held it until at least 1936. It was in 1936 that he and his 12-year-old daughter, Geraldine, stocked the fishless lakes with fish.

The second, and most spectacular, of two waterfalls that drain the lovely Geraldine Lakes.

Looking back at the first Geraldine Lake, and the pond, from the top of the second waterfall.

7. EGYPT LAKE CAMPGROUND

If hiked during the wildflower bloom of the Healy/Simpson meadows, this is one of the most spectacular sights in the Canadian Rockies. The assortment of colours over spacious, undulating hills is utterly breathtaking. The scenery atop Healy Pass is equally impressive, as the 360° panorama of lakes, mountains, meadows and waterfalls can stop backpackers in mid-stride and keep them there for hours. This is a special spot to take off the pack, sit for awhile and take it all in. What's more, the eventual destination of Egypt Lake is a wonderfully charming campground.

DIFFICULTY ▲ ▲ ▲ ▲
DISTANCE: 12.5 KM
ELEVATION GAIN: 630 M (TRAILHEAD TO SUMMIT OF HEALY PASS)

Trailhead:	GPS: N51 06 45.9 W115 46 25.1
	Elevation: 1698 m
Healy Pass Summit:	GPS: N51 05 32.6 W115 51 58.5
	Elevation: 2328 m
Egypt Lake Campground:	GPS: N51 06 06.5 W115 54 03.4
	Elevation: 1995 m

Trailhead: Eight kilometres west of Banff, take the Sunshine Village exit off Highway 1. Travel this picturesque road for 9 km until it reaches the Sunshine Village parking lot. The trailhead is marked at the west end of the gondola terminal.

Mid-July to late August is the preferred season to experience the rolling hills of alpine flowers at Healy Pass. This moderate all-day hike to Egypt Lake utilizes the Healy Creek Valley to travel alongside streams, through forests, across avalanche slopes and ultimately into wildflower meadows.

The first 800 m of this journey is on a broad cat track. Along this stretch of trail, the view across the north side of the valley (over your right

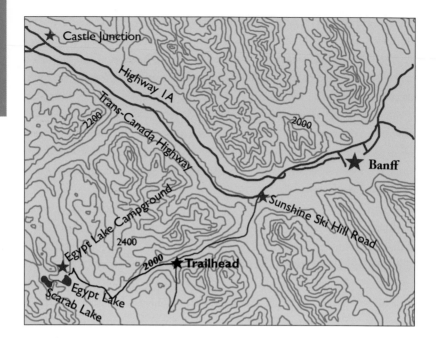

shoulder) consists of a spectacular sheer limestone wall that allows water-falls to plummet several hundred metres to the cliff base. Look slightly more to the east (farther over your right shoulder) to catch a glimpse of Mount Bourgeau (2926 m).

The trail branches to the right off the cat track at 800 m and descends into the Healy Creek Valley; this fork is well marked with signage. The trail descends for a short distance until it reaches a small bridge that crosses the leisurely moving Sunshine Creek. On close examination of this narrow stream, aquatic mosses such as *Scouleria aquatica* can be seen.

From here the trail ascends slowly through a forest of Engelmann spruce and alpine fir. Feathermoss, false azalea and wintergreen inhabit this lovely valley. At 3.1 km the trail crosses Healy Creek to its north bank. The headwaters of this cold, clear stream are only 6–7 km upstream in the alpine ponds at Healy Pass. At 5.5 km you will come upon the Healy Creek campground. This is a valuable resting spot as it contains the only outhouse in the entire valley. Just before reaching this campground, search for the remnants of the foundation of a log cabin along the side of the trail used by John Gerome Healy. This area was explored by him after his arrival in the Rockies in search of precious metals. From the Simpson Pass junction at kilometre 5.9 the trail climbs somewhat more severely but only in spurts. At 7.7 km up the trail you will cross Healy Creek again where the forest opens up into rolling hills of alpine flower meadows. As you ascend farther up into the alpine, the scenery becomes proportionately more stunning. Please stay on the trail to avoid trampling these delicate species of flowers. Alpine anemone, contorted lousewort, bistort, alpine paintbrush and pink heather dominate this lush meadow.

From the summit of Healy Pass, at 9.2 km (2328 m), looking westward, you'll see Whistling Valley below, with Scarab Lake draining into Egypt Lake across the valley. The Pharaoh Peaks are to the northwest (right), with the Ball Range behind that. Twenty-nine kilometres to the southeast at a bearing of 149° true is the unmistakable horn of Mount Assiniboine.

The trail now drops 333 m over the course of the 3.3 km to Pharaoh Creek and the Egypt Lake campground. At the bottom of the descent are a Parks patrol cabin and a junction in the trail. Keep straight on the trail, with the patrol cabin on the right and the Redearth Trail on the left. Crossing Pharaoh Creek here will lead directly to the Egypt Lake campground. The overnight hut at the campground is regulated by Parks Canada and can be reserved ahead of time.

History

The area you are in, Healy Creek and Healy Pass, were named by George M. Dawson in 1884 after Captain John Gerome Healy. In the early 1880s Healy, along with companion J.S. Dennis, decided to try their luck at mining and staking claims in this region, including Healy Creek and Pass, Copper Mountain and Silver City.

Prior to his arrival in the Rockies in search of copper and silver, Healy assisted with the construction of two whisky-running operations, Forts Whoop-up and Hamilton, near present-day Lethbridge, Alberta, in 1869. Prior to that, they had been driven out of Montana for having done the same thing at Fort Benton.

The forts were used to trade cheap whisky to the Natives for thousands of buffalo hides and hundreds of thousands of wolf and fox hides, which were sold at a huge profit. The first of the two Canadian forts was burned down by the Cree in an attempt to save their people from alcoholism, starvation and disease. Shortly after Fort Hamilton was destroyed, a stronger fortification, Fort Whoop-up, was built only a few hundred feet away. This whisky trade was quite possibly the singular reason for the near extinction of the buffalo in Western Canada. In May 1873 the North-West Mounted Police was formed to bring order to a lawless land, and the whisky forts were eventually shut down.

Healy left the Rockies and ventured to the Yukon Territory to join in the Klondike gold rush. He convinced several prominent Chicago families to invest in starting the North American Trading & Transportation Company in Dawson City. The company supplied transportation and supplies to the thousands of prospective millionaires, maintaining a fleet of steamships and supply stores. They were very active in trading furs and gold as well. The company was a huge success and Healy died a very wealthy man.

The naming of Egypt Lake comes from the theme of the surrounding geographical landmarks. The Topographical Survey of Canada came up with these monikers in the early 1900s. The outline of Scarab Lake apparently resembles a beetle, and therefore it was named after the sacred beetle of ancient Egypt. The narrow south section of Mummy Lake should remind you of a mummy's legs and feet, while the entire north portion of the lake is the body and head. Interestingly, the Pharaoh Peaks looked a lot like a row of Egyptian mummies to someone, while Pharaoh Lake speaks for itself with the northwest end appearing like a crowned Pharaoh's head. All of these natural features are in the same vicinity. Regardless of the nomenclature, they are all worth seeing, and the trip should be planned for when the flowers are in full bloom.

The Pharaoh Peaks dominate the western skyline from the summit of Healy Pass.

The spectacular Healy Meadows in full bloom.

The tranquil Egypt Lake.

8. MOSQUITO CREEK CAMPGROUND

Because of its location, removed from both Banff and Jasper, the Mosquito Creek trail has fewer visitors than its counterparts close to the townsites. Combine this with the fact that when you leave the highway and enter the forest, all evidence of civilization immediately disappears; the short 6.4-km hike is genuinely isolated. The best part of this wonderful hike is the last part as you enter the campground, which is in a beautiful valley following the banks of Mosquito Creek. The valley is wide, with sparse tree growth leaving the surrounding mountains in full sight.

DIFFICULTY ▲ ▲
DISTANCE: 6.4 KM
ELEVATION GAIN: 149 M

Trailhead:	GPS: N51 37 48.1 W116 19 42.3
	Elevation: 1837 m
Mosquito Creek Campground:	GPS: N51 39 54.7 W116 18 23.3
	Elevation: 1986 m

Trailhead: At the intersection of the Icefields Parkway and the Trans-Canada Highway, drive north on the parkway for 25 km. Pull into the Mosquito Creek Youth Hostel south of the Mosquito Creek Bridge on the west side of the highway, and park in the designated area for hikers. The trailhead is across the parkway, on the north side of the bridge.

After you cross the pavement and drop down an embankment the trailhead begins without delay. The single track pathway makes its only significant climb right away, venturing up through a forest of lodgepole pine and Engelmann spruce. Lodgepole pine has an extensive range throughout the Rocky Mountains and is thought to be the most common species of pine in these mountains. The ascent does not last long, and soon enough the trail reaches its zenith, levelling off for a quiet walk surrounded by magnificent conifers.

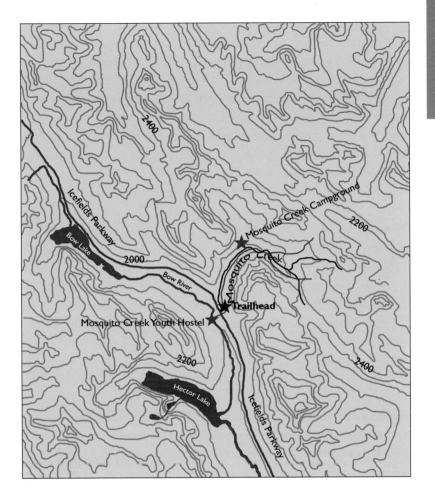

Not soon after you've enjoyed the quiet of the forest, Mosquito Creek begins to speak to you, announcing its presence slightly farther up the trail. The trail breaks through the woods, opening into an expanse featuring the rapidly moving yet shallow Mosquito Creek, making it an archetypical "babbling brook." Just as impressive is the astounding visual impact of the stunning mountains and ridges all around the valley.

Many feeder streams are crossed while tracking Mosquito Creek, and some of the crossings are made of narrow, although flattened, logs.

Extreme caution is advised while walking on these logs in wet conditions. As well, protective rain gear should be worn after a rainfall in a valley such as this, as the moisture from the low, wet foliage will inevitably fall onto pants and boots.

Enjoy the scenery here, because the forest reclaims the trail when it enters Mosquito Creek Campground. The campground offers few luxuries, but even so, a bear pole and outhouse are welcome necessities. There are picnic tables beside the creek, a central cooking and eating area and truly abysmal tent sites.

The only day trip is to venture farther up the trail beyond the campground. Highlights of the trail begin with an alpine stroll above treeline, the small Mosquito Lake, 2.4 km from the campground, North Molar Pass and the upper and lower Fish lakes. There is a campground at Upper Fish Lake. The length of the day trip depends entirely on what you want to see and how high you wish to climb, as the elevation increase from the campground to North Molar Pass is about 600 m over 5.1 km. Lower Fish Lake, the farther of the two, drops 365 m from the summit of North Molar Pass, placing it 9.3 km from Mosquito Creek Campground.

History

Mosquito Creek received official title on May 7, 1959, even though this name had already been used locally for the better part of a century. The derivation of the name is obvious, but it is unknown exactly when it was chosen or who was the first person to be swarmed by mosquitoes in the valley. One thing is certain: there are mosquitoes here. Even during a hike in moderate rains, the little monsters still managed to plague us.

The name Molar Pass comes from Molar Mountain in the same area and received its official status on January 21, 1985. In 1859 James Hector decided that the mountain was tooth-shaped, thus naming it Molar Mountain. The pass was used infrequently as a connecting route from the Pipestone Pass to the Bow Valley.

Above: This young mule deer was spotted with its mother along the Mosquito Creek trail. It was just as curious about us as we were about it. It poked its head through the trees and posed for us for 2–3 minutes before its mother called it in.

Below: Another visitor is met on the way to the Mosquito Creek campground. This Columbia ground squirrel chirped repeatedly to alert his neighbours to our presence in his domain.

The babbling brook called Mosquito Creek.
Fabulous scenery makes the hike in to the
Mosquito Creek Campground an utter pleasure.

9. SKYLINE TRAIL, SNOWBOWL CAMPGROUND

Once out of the forest and above treeline, the skyline trail is a magnificent, wide-open, subalpine meadow augmented by streams and peaks. Although it is a through trail, the most enjoyable portion is from the trailhead at Maligne Lake. Even with an initially substantial elevation rise, the ultimate reward pays huge dividends. The skyline trail is one of the most commonly used trails in Jasper National Park, with through hikers, day hikers, in-and-out backpackers and lodgers staying at Shovel Pass Lodge. Patrons from around the globe frequent Jasper Park specifically to use this trail. It is a rare treat to travel such a tremendous distance above treeline. At times the scenery will genuinely stop you in your tracks.

DIFFICULTY ▲ ▲ ▲
DISTANCE: 12.2 KM (TO CAMPGROUND)
ELEVATION GAIN: 738 M (TO LITTLE SHOVEL PASS)

Trailhead:	GPS: N52 43 35.0 W117 38 41.8
	Elevation: 1692 m
Treeline:	GPS: N52 43 59.2 W117 45 01.5
	Elevation: 2191 m
Little Shovel Pass:	GPS: N52 44 12.8 W117 45 51.7
	Elevation: 2230 m
Snowbowl Campground:	GPS: N52 44 48.6 W117 46 40.6
	Elevation: 2086 m
Big Shovel Pass:	GPS: N52 46 45.3 W117 49 49.8
	Elevation: 2319 m

Trailhead: From the traffic lights at the junction of the Icefields Parkway and Highway 16, drive east on Highway 16 for 6 km to the Maligne Road.

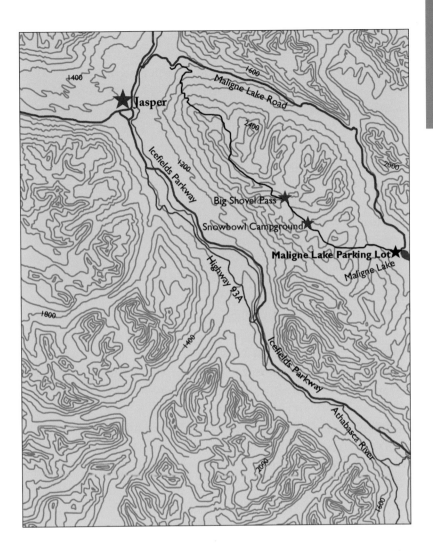

Turn right as soon as you cross the Athabasca River, and stay on the Maligne Lake Road for 45 km to Maligne Lake. Park in the lot on the west side of the lake and look for the trailhead up at the far (north) end of the parking lot, marked "Skyline Trail."

The trail wanders through a forest consisting mainly of the most common pine in the Rockies, lodgepole, and gradually climbs 137 m to Evelyn

Creek Campground. The campground sits just off the trail after crossing Evelyn Creek, 4.8 km from the trailhead. Still in forest, the abrupt ascent to treeline begins as the path rises 362 m within about 3.5 km. As you approach treeline, the trees change to the more stunted subalpine fir with shorter lodgepole pine, and the forest begins thinning out until there is no forest at all. One characteristic of the subalpine fir that is worth mentioning is that the purple cones sit upright on the branch pointing skyward.

The trail climbs steadily above treeline over a vast subalpine meadow dotted with small firs, crossing small valleys and streams. There are many water crossings, mostly bridged, though a couple of them require rock hopping. One in particular declines sharply into a lovely shallow valley with a troublesome deep stream requiring some minor route finding. The elevation gain from treeline to Little Shovel Pass is only 39 m, so the overall change is not really noticeable, especially since the scenery distracts you from any minor differences underfoot.

From Little Shovel Pass to Snowbowl Campground the trail drops 144 m of elevation to 2086 m above sea level. The descent is gradual and again not terribly noticeable. Views along the trail up here include the Queen Elizabeth Range to the east and Antler Mountain to the northwest. Mount Hardisty (2716 m), a peak of the Maligne Range, is situated to the southwest. Snowbowl Campground is 12.2 km from the trailhead, nestled in a cluster of trees slightly off the trail. This is a primitive campground with rough tent pads and an open (no walls or roof), elevated outhouse.

There is still 32 km of hiking to complete the Skyline Trail, so a day trip will take you as far as you wish to go. Big Shovel Pass is 5.3 km farther and climbs only 245 m from the campground. Curator Lake and Shovel Pass Lodge are 8.2 and 9.8 km from the campground respectively.

History

As you step out of your vehicle and wander down to see, touch, hear, taste or smell Maligne Lake, stop for a moment and thank Mary Schäffer for her tremendous, unwavering passion to reinstate this wondrous lake into the protective folds of Jasper National Park. She stood here where you are now, almost 100 years ago and set out over the pass now known as the Skyline Trail.

In 1911, this entire region of lakes, valleys, streams, meadows and mountains was taken away from the park, reducing the area of Jasper National Park to slightly more than 1,000 square miles from its former 5,000 square miles. Dr. D.D. Dowling of the Geological Survey of Canada asked Mrs. Schäffer to lead a survey expedition to the Maligne Lake region to try to reinstate Maligne into the park. Three years earlier Mary had explored Maligne Lake by raft, having named many surrounding features, thus making her the most reliable person to reach the Maligne from Jasper to document and map such an undertaking. And so began her second adventure to Maligne Lake.

Outfitter Jack Otto and his party were hired to make trail for the pack team and surveyors. The decided route over the Maligne Range was to be much quicker and less strenuous than traversing the wilderness of the Maligne Valley. Upon approaching the crest of the pass they discovered that enough snow lingered in mid-June to block the pass. Otto sent a work party to cut a trail through the snow for the rest of the expedition to follow. The snow was so deep that the men found it easier to carve two shovels from spruce trees and shovel their way through. After accomplishing this enormous undertaking, they left the shovels sticking upright in the snow at the summit of the pass to guide the group over the pass. At first Mary Schäffer mistook the shovels for "the thinnest legged sheep" she had ever seen. After realizing what the sheep really were, she agreed to name the pass Shovel Pass.

With the surveying and exploring behind her she devoted the following year to work with the Grand Trunk Pacific and Canadian Pacific railways to have Maligne Lake incorporated back into the park. The railways wanted the tourists and Mrs. Schäffer wanted the area preserved. On June 24, 1912, all of their wishes were granted, as the boundary of Jasper Park was expanded to once more include Maligne Lake.

Mary Townsend Sharples was born on October 4, 1861, in West Chester, Pennsylvania, near Philadelphia. Her family were wealthy Quakers, and she became very highly educated in the Quaker tradition. It was during a CPR trip from Montreal to Vancouver that the Rockies stirred her, and changed her life forever. It was on this same trip that she met Dr. Charles

Schäffer at Glacier House. Schäffer was from Philadelphia as well. They met again back at home and soon married. Returning to the Rockies for 12 consecutive summers, they did not venture far from the rail lines or buggy tracks, but Mary wanted to see more. Charles was 23 years older than Mary and suffered from heart problems that significantly limited their outings. He died in 1903.

With the passing of her parents as well as her husband in 1903, Mary Schäffer retreated to her beloved mountains to finish her husband's book on botany, and from this point forward she would be known as the most adventurous woman in the Canadian Rockies.

The seemingly infinite open expanse of the Skyline Trail.

A peaceful stream meanders through the midst of the Skyline countryside.

10. SATURDAY NIGHT LOOP, MINNOW LAKE CAMPGROUND

This trail has a few names: Saturday Night Lake Loop, Jasper #3 and the Twenty-mile Loop. The loop is actually 27.5 km long and can be done on any night or day that the urge hits. The trail to Minnow Lake Campground is an effortless 10.5-km walk through an interesting forest of lodgepole pine, aspen groves and birch stands. Water is abundant, as the trail is lined with lakes and streams. There are three campgrounds on this trail, but anything beyond Minnow Lake only requires more effort with little more reward, since Minnow Lake Campground is the prettiest setting in this loop. Located 800 m off the main trail, it is very peaceful and the quiet lake is calming.

DIFFICULTY ▲ ▲
DISTANCE: 10.5 KM
ELEVATION GAIN: 324 M

Trailhead: GPS: N52 52 17.8 W118 06 03.8
Elevation: 1092 m

Minnow Lake Campground: GPS: N52 53 22.6 W118 13 21.0
Elevation: 1416 m

Trailhead: From the intersection of Highway 16 and the Icefields Parkway, drive into the township of Jasper. Immediately, the Icefields Parkway becomes Connaught Drive. From the traffic light, drive 1.8 km on Connaught, turn left onto Miette Avenue and go 700 m to the end of Miette Avenue. Turning left here will put you on Pyramid Lake Road, which quickly becomes Cabin Creek Drive behind a mobile home park for 700 m. On the right side of Cabin Creek Drive, across the street from the second of two signs marked "Poplar Avenue," is a short gravel road. A gate at the end says "Water Supply. No Trespassing." Park here. The trailhead is on the left, down the embankment.

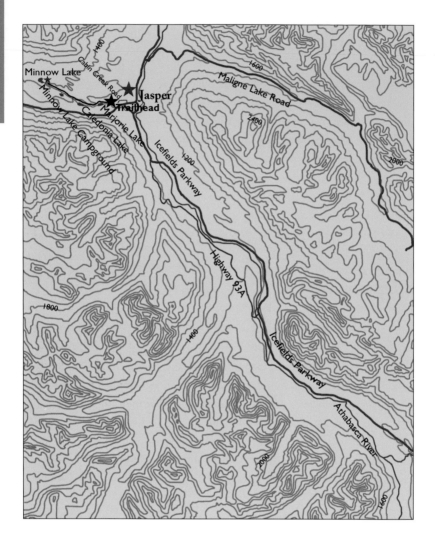

With the trail beginning in a residential area and many locals using it for their morning dog walks, the initial impression is that of traipsing through the suburbs. Nevertheless, within 10 to 15 minutes the locals and the buildings are gone. It is very important to pay close attention to the trail for the first 10 minutes, as there are three junctions and no directional markings. Though the trail is marked with a black-lettered number "3" on a yellow diamond background on the occasional tree. The first junction is within a couple of minutes of the start of the trail, just after you cross Cabin Creek. Turn left here and travel up a short uphill jaunt. Immediately after this, at the top of the little climb, is the second intersection, where the trail continues to the right. Within a few more minutes, the third junction appears, and the correct choice is to veer left.

After 2.5 km of effortless strolling from the trailhead, through open woodland, the trail arrives at Marjorie Lake and runs alongside the length of it. The forest here is reminiscent of a British Columbia Interior forest. This spectacularly clear mountain lake is backdropped by Indian Ridge and Muhigan Mountain, with the latter situated more to the northwest. Two more kilometres beyond here, Caledonia Lake appears through the trees. This lake is considerably larger than Marjorie Lake, at almost 750 m in length. The trail ascends and parallels the eastern shoreline, producing an exceptional downhill view for the length of the lake.

Beyond Caledonia Lake, the trail follows a connector stream and heads into the forest for 20–25 minutes until reaching Small Lake to the left, with a limestone ridge looming over the trail high up on the right.

Fifteen to twenty minutes past Small Lake, and 9.5 km from the trailhead, is the junction to Minnow Lake Campground. Stay left and 800 m of easy going will take you to Minnow Lake Campground. Continuing up to the right for 4 km will bring you to High Lakes Campground, but it pales in comparison to Minnow Lake. This 4-km distance gains 155 m in elevation and is really not worth the effort considering the impressive views bestowed by Minnow Lake.

History

As the exploration and mapping of the Rocky Mountain Parks gave way to tourism development, the Jasper area fell significantly behind the southern regions of Banff and Lake Louise. Most of the responsibility for expanding the trail network and access to the backcountry was shifted to the park wardens. They took over the construction, preservation and overall operation of the trails. An example of these duties was demonstrated by Warden J.A. Rootes's blazing of a rough path from the town of Jasper to

Caledonia Lake in 1913. This was done to promote fishing in the area and was the first recorded exploration into this part of Jasper.

The following year, a Dominion land surveyor, Hugh Matheson, may or may not have discovered Marjorie Lake. Historical information about this trail is sketchy, so it is uncertain whether the original trail cut by Rootes had missed Marjorie Lake. It is also unclear why Matheson gave the lake the name, as apparently, there is no known connection between him and a Marjorie.

This grove of trembling aspen, found just before reaching Marjorie Lake, was an enchanting surprise amid a forest of the usual conifers.

A waterside stroll around Minnow Lake reveals much beauty.

Minnow Lake, looking west from the campground.

The clear, shimmering waters of Marjorie Lake serve as a mirror. These shores are a worthwhile rest stop on the way to Minnow Lake Campground.

11. SOUTH BOUNDARY TRAIL, JACQUES LAKE CAMPGROUND

As an enjoyable day of backpacking, the South Boundary Trail provides impressive companions for most of the hike. The Queen Elizabeth and Colin ranges, on the right and left sides respectively, are in full view until the path darts into the forest about 75 minutes into the hike. The Queen Elizabeth range is the most visible and picturesque of the two. With a wide-open trail for more than half of the walk, minimal elevation gain, lakeside exposure and spectacular mountain ranges framing the valley, this hike is one to appreciate and enjoy. Stop and take pictures, or stop and look in awe, but be sure you stop to enjoy. Of the entire 167 km of the South Boundary Trail, this first 12.2 km is possibly the most scenic and enjoyable.

DIFFICULTY ▲ ▲ ▲
DISTANCE: 12.2 KM
ELEVATION GAIN: 78 M

Trailhead:	GPS: N52 50 57.8 W117 43 19.9
	Elevation: 1445 m
Junction at First Summit Lake:	GPS: N52 53 01.7 W117 45 02.5
	Elevation: 1523 m
Jacques Lake Campground:	GPS: N52 56 00.8 W117 44 18.8
	Elevation: 1492 m

Trailhead: From the traffic lights at the junction of the Icefields Parkway and Highway 16, drive east on Highway 16 for 6 km to the Maligne Lake Road. After crossing the Athabasca River, immediately turn left and drive another 28 km. The pull-off is on the left side, marked as the "South Boundary Trail."

The path begins as a spacious trail. You pass a cabin and corral within the first few minutes. Fifteen minutes later the south shore of Beaver Lake

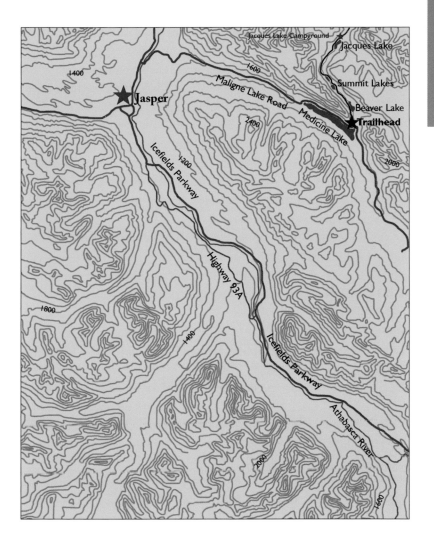

with its boats and boat launch are passed. The trail then sidesteps the lake for several scenic minutes. Beyond the lake the trail continues to offer incredible, neck-craning panoramas of the Queen Elizabeth and Colin ranges. This lasts for 2 km of easy trekking until the path emerges from the forest onto a hillside of small brush and vegetation devoid of trees, thus permitting much grander views of the parallel mountain ranges.

The first of the Summit Lakes is met at the distal end of the brush field at a marked fork in the trail. Follow the trail marked "South Boundary Trail" to the right onto a narrow path into a dank coniferous forest. The trail is unchanged for the remainder of the hike, with intermittent gaps in the trees allowing you to see the Summit Lakes. The left option of the fork sends the trail along the shoreline of the first lake, but there is some difficulty recovering the main trail since there is not a distinct path heading back to it. So, some bushwhacking will be necessary if you choose this alternative. A quick trip down the left fork toward the lake should be taken for a relaxing break, as it provides views of the surrounding mountains that are even more impressive.

The trail winds its way around trees in the forest for another 4–5 km. Just when you have had enough of tripping over myriad exposed roots, the trail emerges on the south bank of Jacques Lake. At the far (north) end of the lake lies the campground in a wonderful setting back from the lake.

History

Jacques Lake, Jacques Creek, the Jacques Range and Roche Jacques all take their names from Jacques Cardinal, a Métis employee of the North West Company during the 1820s and '30s. Mount Cardinal was named after Jacques in 1922. All of these natural features are located in Jasper National Park, for this is where Cardinal did most of his work and trading. His main duty was to provide horses to the fur traders, but evidently he became an avid trader himself.

South Boundary Trail was the chosen trading route to the Brazeau Valley for Cardinal. Others followed this path, including the infamous botanist David Douglas, who inaccurately recorded the heights of Mounts Brown and Hooker at somewhere between 15,000 and 17,000 feet above sea level. It would take an exploration 66 years later to realize that these were not the tallest mountains in North America, and that they were only 9,184 and 10,781 feet high respectively (see Fortress Lake). On an outing in the Athabasca Pass, Douglas set off alone and soon became lost somewhere along the Whirlpool River. He was lucky to spot "... curling blue smoke issuing from trees..." He had come across the encampment of Jacques Cardinal, who was delivering horses up Athabasca Pass to Douglas's camp. Cardinal invited Douglas into his hut for dinner, while expedition leader Edward Ermatinger was in a state of "distress" until he found the hut and Douglas.

It is uncertain which of the Cardinals the Cardinal River was named for. It is widely believed it was Jacques, though documentation of the Métis peoples at the time was not very accurate. Nevertheless, Jacques Cardinal is buried along the banks of Cardinal River.

Above: This unoccupied Parks Canada cabin was nestled in a meadow with a backdrop of snow-capped peaks on the way to Jacques Lake.

Below: The Colin Range near the Summit Lakes of the South Boundary Trail.

Beaver Lake with the Queen Elizabeth Range in the background.

12. LAKE MINNEWANKA, AYLMER PASS CAMPGROUND (LM 8)

Although the elevation of the trailhead and the campground are almost identical, the journey between these two points is not a breezy lakeside stroll. Even so, the hike climbs to a maximum of only 62 m, and becomes more of a hillside stroll, eventually dropping down to the lakeshore again. The 7.8-km hike to the campground continuously exposes you to several different perspectives of Lake Minnewanka against the backdrop of the Fairholme Range, including Mounts Inglismaldie and Girouard as they skirt the south shoreline.

Day tripping from campground LM 8 includes either exploring the trail farther up the lake or the 800-m upward climb to Aylmer Lookout.

DIFFICULTY ▲ ▲
DISTANCE: 7.8 KM
ELEVATION GAIN: 62 M

Trailhead:	GPS: N51 15 09.6 W115 29 41.4
	Elevation: 1500 m
Lake Minnewanka Summit:	GPS: N51 15 22.6 W115 28 48.1
	Elevation: 1562 m
Aylmer Pass Campground:	GPS: N51 16 48.7 W115 24 39.6
	Elevation: 1502 m

Trailhead: Park in the spacious Lake Minnewanka parking lot, 5.5 km north of the intersection of the Trans-Canada Highway and Lake Minnewanka Road, at the east gate to the Banff townsite. Walk the pavement past the concession stand on the left and a covered picnic area farther up the trail on the right. Pick up the sign with the graphic of the hiker on it directing you to the trailhead.

The trail begins as a wide walk alongside the picturesque lake that is twenty-four km in length with depths of up to 142 m. It is the longest lake

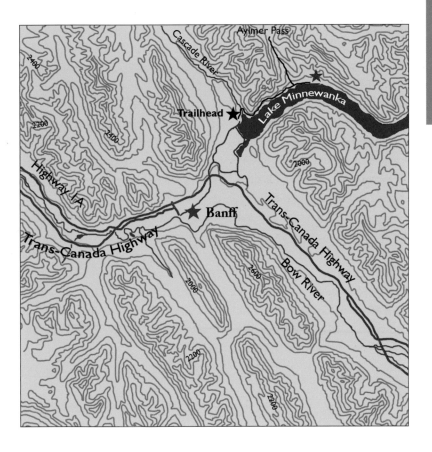

in the Rocky Mountain Parks system. Within ten minutes, the trail enters a forest of lodgepole pine, briefly leaving the lakeside to take you around a large bay where the Cascade River enters the lake. Watch for a fork in the trail and the marker to campground LM 8, your destination, to the right. Continue along this route until the trail reaches the sturdy bridge crossing the Cascade River, one of many delights presented on this hike. When the water is clear and undisturbed, the sharp, flat limestone banks are visible to a substantial depth.

The trail is evident, but keep an eye out for the official Parks Canada name of Campground LM 8, not Aylmer Pass Campground. Some 30–35 minutes into the hike the path begins its climb, soon reaching its apex at

1562 m, N51 15 22.6 W115 28 48.1. Looking to the north (left) at a magnificent bluff with many great slabs eroded away, it is soon understood why the trail is a trek on loose rubble. In due course the elevation is lost as once more the trail drops down close to the lake.

After an hour and a half of hiking, you enter an exposed aspen and birch grove with a hillside on the left that is devoid of trees. This simply adds to the overall appeal of this trip. Five minutes later the deciduous stand merges back into conifers and the path crosses a small river. The rest of the hike is a walk of a little over a kilometre, skirting the lake through forest to the campground.

Aylmer lookout is the best day trip from the campground, and begins as a 2.3-km hike with an elevation gain of almost 600 m. This is a steep grade and not for the faint of heart. At 2.3 km a sign will guide you to the right for another 1.7-km hike to the Aylmer Lookout, built in 1946 as one of seven fire lookouts in Banff National Park. If you still have some energy, go back to the junction, turn right and climb upward for another 3.4 km to reach the crest of Aylmer Pass, at 2287 m. This a total elevation gain of nearly 800 m in 5.6 km. An amazing workout.

History

In 1888 the original name of either Devil's Head Lake or Devil's Lake was replaced by the Department of the Interior to the more tourist friendly one of Minnewanka. "Minnewanka," translated from the Stoney, means "Lake of the water spirit." The original moniker came by way of a Stoney legend of a half-man, half-fish creature that inhabited the lake, victimizing innocent boaters.

Many years before, in 1841, Sir George Simpson called the lake "Peechee" after his Métis guide, whose name was actually spelled "Piché." However, the name was never official and did not appear on any maps or documents. During a cross-continent trip in 1884, Dr. G.M. Dawson named a peak at the south end of the lake Mount Peechee in honour of the same Métis guide, though Piché himself was not on this trip with Dawson.

Mount Aylmer was named by J.J. McArthur in 1890 to immortalize his hometown of Aylmer, Quebec, which in turn was named for Matthew Whitworth-Aylmer, Fifth Baron Aylmer (1775–1850), who served as both

Governor General of British North America and Lieutenant Governor of Lower Canada from 1831 to 1835.

During the late 1800s and early 1900s the northwest end of Lake Minnewanka was a resort community called Minnewanka Landing. It was situated near the present-day tourist area, and consisted of hotels, wharves, cottage lots and cottages and restaurants. Boat tours and sailing excursions were also offered. As a popular resort community in close proximity to Banff townsite, the place needed an improved shoreline to spruce up its appeal, so a wooden dam was constructed on Devil's Creek, which accomplished this goal at least for awhile.

In 1912, a second dam was built, this time in Devil's Canyon, for the purpose of water storage, thus creating another new shoreline by raising the lake level by 3.5 m. The consequence of this action was the flooding of Devil's Creek. This was not enough for poor Lake Minnewanka, though, as the federal government constructed a power plant in 1923 to supply electricity to Banff, and finally, in 1941, the present-day dam was built under the War Measures Act. The final dam raised the water level by an astounding 30 m, extending the lake an additional 8 km in length and flooding the entire town of Minnewanka Landing.

Today the submerged remains of the town are used for recreational scuba diving, with Parks Canada supplying detailed maps, buoys, markers and interpretations of the entire town and the various bridges and dams.

The Cascade River beneath a bridge crossing as it enters Lake Minnewanka.

Looking south down Lake Minnewanka from the high point of the trail.

13. FORTRESS LAKE TRAIL, BIG BEND CAMPGROUND

This campground may very well have the most spectacular setting of any back-country campground in the entire Rocky Mountain park system.

The wide trail does not offer much viewing through the trees, but it is only a little more than 6 km of level hiking to the campground. The trail continues to Fortress Lake, but going there is not recommended unless you expect to get aw-fully wet. Crossing the Chaba River requires fording cold water that is one-half to two metres deep. Even in low-water season there is still a very dangerous risk of being swept away in the strong current.

Day tripping to the Athabasca Crossing Campground and the Athabasca River bridge will take most of a day, as they are 8.8 and 9.3 km up the trail respectively.

DIFFICULTY ▲
DISTANCE: 6.3 KM
ELEVATION GAIN: 105 M

Trailhead: GPS: N52 31 57.7 W117 38 43.5
                      Elevation: 1408 m

Big Bend Campground: GPS: N52 29 08.1 W117 39 18.7
                      Elevation: 1303 m

Trailhead: From the intersection of Highway 16 and the Icefields Parkway travel 53.5 km south to the Sunwapta Falls parking lot. Look for the throng of tourists making their way to and from the Sunwapta Falls viewpoint bridge. Break trail through the cameras to arrive, hopefully unscathed, at the far end of the short bridge. Actually, the falls are quite spectacular, justifying the heavy traffic. Stop and take a look yourself.

After you cross the bridge over Sunwapta Falls, you'll see the huge crowd of tourists suddenly thin out, as not many visitors to the falls venture farther than the bridge. Within 20 minutes the trail becomes wet as it passes over what appears to be a permanently soggy forest floor. This is

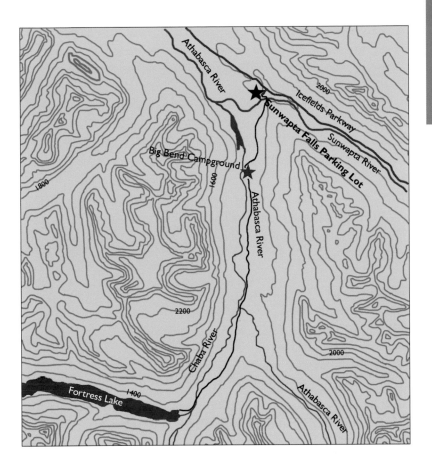

confirmed by a corduroy of logs that extends through the forest for about 500 to 750 m. Stay on this track, as the sidelines can make your cozy, dry, warm boots suddenly very wet and cold.

Another 15 minutes gets you across a small stream. The level, uneventful, well-trodden path reaches through the beautiful coniferous forest, and soon enough the 6 km is complete as the spectacular sight of the big bend in the Athabasca River comes into full view. As the forest opens up at Big Bend the most prominent sight is Mount Quincy standing directly south 16.5 km away. Because of the flat walk-in, the work is done in 75 to 90 minutes, allowing hikers to pack in a few extra luxuries. These peaceful,

101

tranquil, rapid waters can quickly calm even the most bad-tempered individuals. The waters here move slow enough to become entrancing, yet just fast enough to make pre-whitewater bubbling sounds, thus momentarily breaking the enchanting trance.

Day hiking the trail is much like the first 6 km except that there is a mild rise in elevation immediately after leaving Big Bend Campground. One to two kilometres later the trail loses the elevation gained and drops down to the Athabasca River. Then, just as quickly, it regains the forest. The rest of the hike is straightforward by simply following the main trail. There are no key intersections or diversions. The Athabasca River bridge is a wondrous destination, since it has few lingering visitors, leaving it for your sole enjoyment. Quiet contemplation on this structure makes this long day trip meaningful.

History

Like many natural landmarks in the Rockies, Fortress Lake was discovered during a quest for something else. Arthur Philemon Coleman, a professor of geology from the University of Toronto, his brother, L. Quincy Coleman, a rancher from Morley, Alberta, and L.B. Stewart, also a professor from the University of Toronto, all set out in the summer of 1893 to find and climb the tallest mountains in North America. There was a legend floating around that Mounts Hooker and Brown were both between 15,000 and 17,000 feet above sea level.

This written report had come 66 years earlier from the Scottish botanist David Douglas after he travelled through Athabasca Pass in 1827. Douglas named the peaks on this voyage. The Colemans and Stewart would eventually discover that these mountains came up well short of their celebrated status, with Mount Brown a mere 9,184 feet and Hooker only slightly taller at 10,781 feet. In fact, it was Douglas who recorded the first ascent of Mount Brown in 1827 and declared he had accomplished this feat in an afternoon. So, it is still a bit of a mystery why he claimed it to be 17,000 feet high. Mount Hooker was conquered almost a century later, in 1924, by Conrad Kain, J. Monroe Thorington, Alfred J. Ostheimer and M.M. Strumia.

During the mountain finding mission the threesome named a mountain that was like a great buttress, calling it Fortress Mountain. The pass and lake take their names from the mountain. A.P. Coleman also gave the Chaba River its name, as he noticed while following this stream that there were countless beaver dams in the river, as well as trees cut down by beaver alongside the river. "Chaba" comes from the Stoney Indian word for beaver. Fortress Lake was not visited until four years later, by Walter Wilcox and Robert L. Barrett. Mary Schäffer also took an exploration party to this beautiful lake in 1907.

Above: Still waters from the Athabasca River linger beside Big Bend Campground. Dragon Peak in the background.

Below: Mount Quincy looms high over the Athabasca River looking south from Big Bend campground

103

14. ATHABASCA PASS, WHIRLPOOL CAMPGROUND

Whirlpool Campground is primitive, as it is not spacious and is barely off the trail. There are no marked campsites and no tables, with only a bear pole straddled high between two trees (bring your own rope) and a privy for a restroom. However, the serene setting of the Whirlpool River will soon put all this lack of luxury out of your mind. The trail is a 6.5 km hike to the campground with a total elevation gain of no more than 70 m.

A long day trip from this campsite will take you to the historic remains of the Old Tie Camp, which in the 1910s was used by the Otto brothers for making railway ties. Remnants of the camp include lumber from boats, cabins and the mill and scrap metal from cans and tools.

DIFFICULTY ▲ ▲ ▲

DISTANCE: 6.5 KM

ELEVATION GAIN: 67 M

Trailhead:	GPS: N52 40 10.6 W117 57 15.9
	Elevation: 1217 m
Summit of trail:	GPS: N52 39 33.9 W117 57 07.4
	Elevation: 1284 m
Whirlpool Campground:	GPS: N52 37 36.4 W117 59 35.2
	Elevation: 1242 m

Trailhead: From the intersection of Highway 16 and the Icefields Parkway (Highway 93) drive south for 30 km until you reach the Athabasca Falls turnoff on the right side of the highway. This in turn will place you on Highway 93A. Stay on this roadway for 8.6 km, going past the Athabasca Falls parking lot turnoff on the left, to the Moab Lake intersection. Turn left. The remainder of the drive is now on a very dusty gravel road lasting 7.0 km, though the posted distance reads 7.5 km. The Moab Lake parking lot is the trailhead for this adventure.

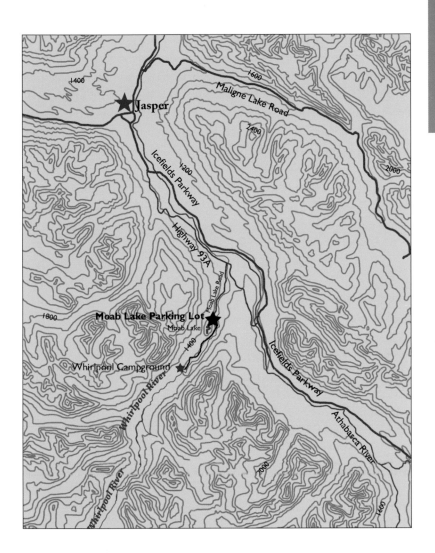

From the parking lot the trail begins as a single-track trail into a tight forest. Immediately, the trail crosses the Moab Lake outlet stream and quickly rises to head toward Moab Lake. For another 750 m the trail remains narrow until it opens up at the Moab Lake junction. From here, the path becomes a double-track obsolete fire road that has become overgrown over the years since being downgraded to a hiking trail. Looking down the trail from here, scenery of mountain peaks and ridges starts to come into full view. Over your right shoulder the devastating effects of lightning are evident as the residue of a forest fire ignited in 2000 are in plain view. Moab Lake is down the trail to the right. This is a favorite fishing spot for many of the locals. However, to reach Whirlpool Campground, continue straight down the main track. The remainder of the trip persists as an open trail meandering effortlessly with minimal changes in elevation. Eventually a corrugated culvert is encountered about 750 m before the campground. Look closely into the bush for the campground sign, as it is hidden slightly off-trail behind overgrown tree branches. The only other indication of the campground is a faint, narrow path directly off the left side of the main trail.

Although the campground is not extraordinary, the scenery certainly is. A range of mountain peaks separating the Whirlpool River and Geraldine Lakes lying in the next valley to the southeast occupies the horizon directly across the river. At this site the Whirlpool River widens, creating eddies, stillness and even marshes at low water.

The day trip on this excursion is an additional 8 km of easy hiking from Whirlpool Campground. The fire road continues for 2 km until it reaches a single-track tributary trail off to the right into the bush. Continuing straight on the fire road ends within 25–30 m, leaving no doubt that the preferred route is into the forest. The remaining 6 km is a path which opens periodically to offer the occasional panorama. The trail makes its way past Tie Campground at the 11.3-km mark. This should not be confused with the historic Old Tie Camp, which is 2.2 km farther up the trail.

History

Athabasca Pass was discovered by David Thompson in 1811 after the Peigan Indians prohibited travel through Howse Pass in 1810. The Peigan had become particularly hostile toward white men after their defeat by Native enemies who had been equipped with firearms supplied by white traders. With Howse Pass closed by the Peigan to thwart further trade, Thompson's new pass became the main fur trade route over the Rockies.

Thompson set out on October 29, 1810, leaving Boggy Hall with the largest contingent of manpower in his renowned career. The party consisted of three women, 25 men and 24 horses. Among the party was William Henry, as clerk, and an Iroquois guide known as Thomas, who would direct the group over the pass. Henry would eventually leave the expedition and set up a supply line from a post on the Athabasca River.

After months of gruelling challenges, horrible weather, frustrated companions and impossible terrain, they arrived at the northernmost point of the Big Bend of the Columbia River on January 19, 1811. By now all but five men had left the team. Two stayed with Thompson to construct a building to wait out the winter while three more returned for supplies. On February 17 the three men returned to "Boat Encampment," the name given by Thompson and his men to the winter settlement, to spend the next two months constructing a canoe.

Traders using the pass departed the North Saskatchewan River and travelled cross county to the Athabasca River. After passing Jasper House, the pass ventured up the Whirlpool River. From the summit the trail made its way to the Canoe River by way of the Wood River and finally to the Big Bend of the Columbia.

Although the pass was difficult to cross (it was declared as "not fit for horses") and was out of the way because it was so far north, it was all that was available at the time. There were rumours of Kootenay Indian crossings, though these were not confirmed until many years later. So it was that Athabasca Pass became the main route for almost 50 years.

An open meadow in an immense forest just off the Athabasca Pass Trail.

Whirlpool Peak at the Moab Lake junction of the Athabasca Trail.

The northwest lateral flank of Whirlpool Peak from the Whirlpool campground.

The Whirlpool River relaxes as it passes by the campground.

109

15. SPRAY RIVER CAMPGROUND (SP6)

With 4.5 to 5.0 km to hike on a flat, wide fire road, the Spray River Campground is ideal for an early season warm-up trip or a late fall hike before the heavy snow begins to fly. There are only a couple of stretches with nominal elevation change, making this one of the easiest backpacking jaunts in the Rockies. Because of this, the trip is most enjoyable and the wide trail can be shared with friends walking side by side.

This is part of the Spray River Loop, which is 12 to 15 km long, going up one side of the Spray River, crossing the river and travelling down the other side. One end is located at the Banff Springs golf course, the other behind the Fairmont Banff Springs Hotel parkade. This route begins at the golf course end of the trail.

DIFFICULTY ▲
DISTANCE: 4.5–5.0 KM
PEAK ELEVATION: 1484 M

Trailhead:	GPS: N51 09 53.8 W115 33 29.6
	Elevation: 1370 m
Spray River Campground (Sp6):	GPS: N51 07 33.6 W115 31 45.1
	Elevation: 1421 m

Trailhead: The parking lot for the trailhead is at the Bow Falls parking lot. From the Banff townsite drive across the Bow River bridge at the south end of Banff Avenue. Turn left onto Spray River Road and drive 750 m to Bow Falls Avenue on the left. Turn down here to the Bow Falls parking lot.

After checking out the falls, walk across the narrow Spray River Bridge. As soon as the bridge is crossed, there is a trail on the right skirting the upper edge of the 15th fairway. This trail is here for the purpose of crossing the golf course without running across the middle of the fairway, so be sure to cross here and not farther down. This is the same route taken to pick up the Mount Rundle trailhead. Staying on this trail along the edge

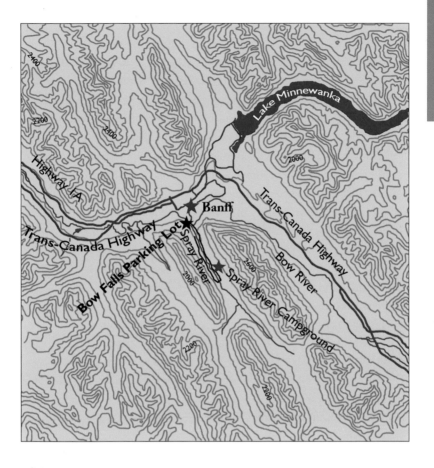

of the 15th fairway, now on the other side, will direct you to the Spray River/Mount Rundle signage within a few moments.

Throughout the journey there are two sets of signs, old and new, with identical markers but differing distances. So, from this intersection, turn right and begin trekking either 4.6 or 4.9 km to Campground Sp6. The fire road trail begins to climb now but maintains this mild ascent for only five minutes or so. It then levels off and really does not change much until the approach to the campground. Numerous signs dot the early part of the trail, but regardless, they all steer you to Sp6 along the main fire road. Horses and cyclists share the main route, so it can become mucky in spots, but the surrounding forest of Engelmann spruce, lodgepole pine and standing birch is sparse, permitting off-trail travel around some of the worst spots.

At any time along the way, the view of the Spray River down below is accessible just off the road to the right. Sulphur Mountain and its tram are also visible from the high banks over the Spray River. This short, easy hike will begin a very quick and limited descent about ten minutes before reaching the campground. The trail drops just enough to reach the same level as the river. Spray River Campground is unique in that it is stretched out along a narrow strip of forest abutting a hillside on the left side of the trail. The bear pole and cooking area are reached first, and the tent pads are two minutes up the trail, with an outhouse in between.

There is not much for day trips from here other than simply spending the day exploring the Spray River or relaxing on its beaches. A beautiful location such as this requires suppression of all peripheral influences in order to allow an endless day of nothingness. The loop can be completed on the way out instead of returning the same way, though it consists of much of the same strolling among conifer trees.

History

The name has been used for the river and valley since 1885, although it is uncertain who gave it the name. It is a descriptive term coming from the spray emitted from Bow Falls where the Spray meets the Bow River.

Sulphur Mountain on the opposite side of the river, glimpsed while trekking the Spray River trail.

16. TAYLOR LAKE CAMPGROUND (TA6)

Although 602 m of elevation is gained to reach Taylor Lake, it feels like much less, as the grade is spread out over 6.3 km and is achieved with long, level runs between switchbacks. With stream and bog crossings being the only natural landmarks through a forest of lodgepole pine and Engelmann spruce, the journey to the lake is uneventful. The setting of the lake – with a waterfall inlet stream at the far end and the surrounding peaks of Mount Bell to the left and Panorama Ridge to the right – is mesmerizing.

DIFFICULTY ▲ ▲ ▲
DISTANCE: 6.3 KM
ELEVATION GAIN: 602 M

Trailhead: GPS: N51 18 28.9 W116 01 26.7
                                  Elevation: 1475 m

Taylor Lake Campground (Ta6):   GPS: N51 17 52.3 W116 05 19.2
                                  Elevation: 2077 m

Trailhead: Drive west from Castle Junction for 8.2 km or east from Lake Louise for 20 km to the Taylor Lake parking lot on the south side of the Trans-Canada Highway.

The trail immediately crosses Taylor Creek, which is the outlet stream for Taylor Lake, with the trailhead sign displayed on the other side. The path enters the forest at this point and does not emerge until it approaches Taylor Lake. It begins as a level, single-track trail with some rock and root exposure.

Within the first kilometre another bridge crosses the same stream again and remains with you for a great deal of the trek. The route now begins its gradual climb, and from here on in it continues to climb very insidiously, with intermittent plateaus. Even though the stream does not stay close to the trail, it is certainly within earshot, but 30 to 40 minutes into the hike the trail departs the sound of the stream and suddenly the

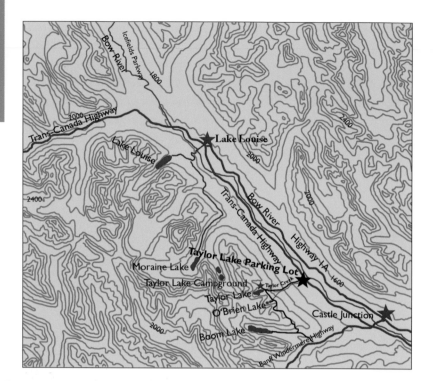

forest is silent. It is a remarkable transformation. You are really not aware of how loud the stream was until it is gone.

Another ten minutes beyond the bridge brings the trail to the first of two short, dilapidated boardwalks crossing a bog. The second one is another 40 minutes away and contains two galvanized drain pipes. From here, there is only another 20 to 25 minutes of backpacking to go. Taylor Creek is crossed for a third time just prior to rising to the open, flat, mushy meadow of Taylor Lake. Crossing this soggy meadow requires some skilled manoeuvring to remain dry. Follow the sign to Campground Ta6.

The campground sits level on the shore of the lake, containing a bear pole and an outhouse. It is a place of silence and splendour. Having mountain peaks looming on both sides and an opening between them at the far end, the lake is iridescent yet clear, with many surrounding features available to reflect in it. Even the outlet area is still and clear.

For day adventures, return to the main trail to find the sign that directs the trail toward O'Brien and Boom lakes. The trail to these lakes is lined with forest, with a couple of small wildflower meadows. The much smaller O'Brien Lake is encountered first, at 2.1 km from Taylor Lake, while Boom Lake is much farther, at 7.5 km. If Boom Lake is on your list, it would be a much quicker trip from its own trailhead on the Banff-Windermere Highway (Highway 93 south). The distance in is only 5.1 km.

History

Taylor Lake draws its name from George Herbert Taylor, who worked as a packer for A.O. Wheeler during Wheeler's employ with the Dominion Topographic Survey. It is unknown who named the lake or when.

The name of nearby O'Brien Lake does not have a definitive origin, thought it is thought the lake may have been named after a particular CPR section supervisor.

Taylor Creek as it exits Taylor Lake.

115

The mist above Taylor Lake barely hides the limestone
cliffs of Mount Bell. The lake is fed by a waterfall at the
far end of the lake.

The weather beneath the clouds was a mixture of
drizzling rain and snow. The last 150 metres to the
summit of Ha Ling Peak was spectacular.

Chapter 6
Scrambling Trips

1. PANORAMA RIDGE

The scramble to the summit of this ridge promises hard work on loose scree, and wet feet while fording Babel Creek. The only way to prevent the fulfillment of either promise is to take the much longer route via Taylor Lake, but this route is easier and quicker.

Achieving any of the adventures in this guidebook is accomplished by using our finite amount of time to do this instead of doing something else. Even when taking into account the cursed scree slopes, fording rivers, walking countless kilometres through forest and balancing on a precarious summit ridge, the thought of wanting to do anything other than this is strikingly strange. So, enjoy the scree and the river crossing, because the euphoria at the summit is just irreplaceable. Moreover, when you are sitting at home this will now become the only thing you think about and all you want to do.

DIFFICULTY ▲ ▲ ▲
ELEVATION GAIN: 905 M

Trailhead:	GPS: N51 19 43.3 W116 10 54.0
	Elevation: 1873 m
Panorama Ridge:	GPS: N51 19 34.3 W116 08 04.6
	Elevation: 2778 m
Summit:	GPS: N51 18 24.1 W116 07 15.2
	Elevation: 2834 m

Trailhead: From the Lake Louise village drive up Lake Louise Drive toward the Chateau and turn left on Moraine Lake Road. Continue to the Moraine Lake parking lot, approximately 12 km from the turnoff. Find the trail on the south side of the lot behind the public toilets. The trail

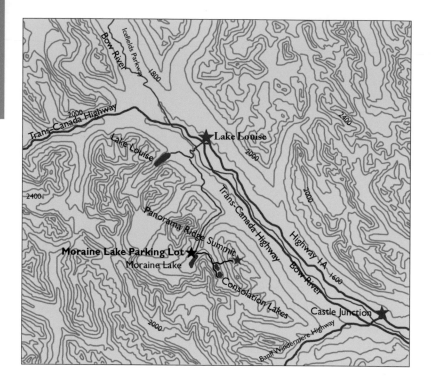

crosses the Moraine Lake outlet stream and intersects a fork in the trail without delay. The way is clear, as signs will direct you to the left toward Consolation Lakes 2.9 km up the main trail. There is a 65 m elevation gain over the course of this 2.9-km hike.

There is a short expanse of boulder hopping for a few minutes as you traverse an avalanche slope. Upward to the right is a splendid view of the Tower of Babel. The trail now enters a forest of spruce and fir that parallels Babel Creek until approaching the lower reaches of Lower Consolation Lake. When the trail breaks through the forest it is greeted by a meadow of wildflowers and a clear look at the route up Panorama Ridge lying across the creek to the left.

Upon arriving here, begin searching for a narrow, shallow area for crossing the creek. The creek seems to narrow near the lake, but this may change from year to year. The water is only knee-deep at most, but it is still advisable to seek shallow water, as there is a bit of a current. There are remnants of a makeshift crossing constructed of logs, rocks and other debris, but this is now unsafe. The water is painfully cold and the rocks are hard on bare feet, so neoprene water boots are highly recommended.

On the other side, after a brief encounter with a boulder field, you'll find the trail evident and well marked. As with most scree slopes there are many trails, with sometimes one being better than the rest. Try to search out the most frequented, packed-down path if possible. Again, this may change from one year to another. Regardless, this is going to be a struggle even if a packed trail is found. However, since the mountainside is barren, the scenery is fantastic during the entire trip, so listen to your legs and stop frequently to turn around and take a look. Otherwise you really will be missing the point of being here. Directly below are Consolation Valley and the lakes, and across the valley is the Tower of Babel, Mount Babel and Mount Fay. Mount Temple is in full view 5.7 km to the northwest.

The incline becomes slightly steeper close to the top, but not for long. The ridge and summit are composed of rock and boulders, making the ridge walk somewhat annoying. If you are not happy with the top of the ridge as your summit, then toil over the boulders for another 1.8 km to reach the true summit 56 m higher.

History

Consolation Valley Trail, which leads to the trailhead of Panorama Ridge, was first explored and then named by Walter Wilcox and Ross Peacock in 1899. There is not much information available about that expedition, but written records show they named this valley as a contrast to the neighbouring "Desolation Valley." Desolation Valley, given its name by Samuel E.S. Allen, would be renamed Valley of the Ten Peaks a short time later. Wilcox wrote, "We were very much pleased with the place, and Ross suggested that, since the other was called Desolation Valley, we might call this 'Consolation Valley,' a name that seemed quite appropriate."

Panorama Ridge derives its name from the spectacular view from the summit, but there are no records of who named the ridge or when it received its name.

Consolation Lakes from the top of Panorama Ridge.

Amazing easterly view while strolling along the top of Panorama Ridge.

The approach to the summit of Panorama Ridge is straightforward: just up.

2. OBSERVATION PEAK

Looking up at this mountain from the highway, it seems as though the peak is in full view, but the summit that is seen from the highway, and the base of the mountain, is actually the false summit. The true summit lies an additional 15–20 minutes northeast (left and behind) and 106 m higher from the false summit. From either summit, the view is absolutely captivating. The mesmerizing sight of peaks, turquoise waters, glaciers, waterfalls, rivers and valleys is both enlightening and calming. This is one of the few peaks in the region that is over the magic 10,000-foot height.

DIFFICULTY ▲ ▲
ELEVATION GAIN: 1102 M

| Trailhead: | GPS: N51 43 13.1 W116 29 40.2 |
| | Elevation: 2072 m |

| False Summit: | GPS: N51 44 07.8 W116 28 01.9 |
| | Elevation: 3010 m |

| Observation Peak Summit: | GPS: N51 45 31.8 W116 28 00.9 |
| | Elevation: 3176 m |

Trailhead: Starting at the interchange of the Trans-Canada Highway and the Icefields Parkway, head north on the Icefields Parkway for 40.5 km to the Bow Summit. Pull over on the east (right) side of the highway onto a gravel road and park.

Of the two drainage avalanche gullies visible from the highway, travel up the right side of the left gully. This eventually climbs up onto a ridge between the two gullies that takes you to the false summit and eventually the true summit.

From the highway walk the old road as it veers left and quickly narrows into a trail. Within five to ten minutes you'll come to a cairn marking the trail off the road. Step east (right) into the bush and follow the

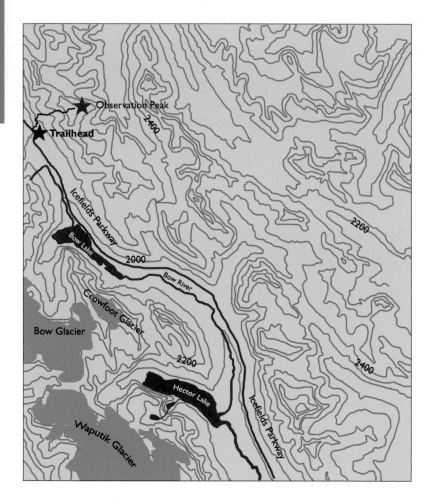

occasionally faint trail through the forest for another 5–10 minutes until it opens up into a drainage gully. Follow the trail on the right side of this gully, keeping an eye on well-placed cairns.

The way is uneventful until halfway up the ridge, where there is a moderate section of scrambling that requires some patience. Again, look for cairns to the right to find the easiest route around this rock band. Otherwise, this minor inconvenience can simply be worked around with little difficulty by climbing over it. Beyond this rock band the trail becomes a scree slope for the remaining 400 m to the false summit. It appears that many earlier scramblers have also had difficulty with this scree slope, as there are numerous trails crisscrossing the slope in an effort to minimize the relentless backward sliding caused by climbing such an incline of rock debris. The easiest way up is to search out the most trampled route and stick to it.

Upon reaching the false summit, take a break from the scree and reap the reward. A sight so beautiful may not come your way ever again. Gaze across the Icefields Parkway to see the incredible turquoise waters of Peyto and Bow lakes. In the background behind these lakes are the toes of the Crowfoot Glacier and the massive Peyto Glacier, which is an extension of the much larger Wapta Icefield. Mount Jimmy Simpson to the southwest and Caldron Peak, behind Peyto Lake, are just two of the noteworthy peaks in full view from the false summit.

Dipping down into a saddle and ascending up a gentle slope out of the saddle in a northerly direction, the trail takes you to the true summit in 15–20 minutes.

History

After climbing many mountains in this area, Rev. C.L. Noyes and his party realized that this peak offered some of the best panoramas in the area and named Observation Peak in 1899. During an expedition of climbing and exploring the Bow Lake region, Noyes, along with fellow clergyman Rev. Harry P. Nicholls and lawyer Charles S. Thompson, climbed this peak while the two other members of their party, guide Ralph Edwards and another lawyer, George Weed, ventured northward to find a shortcut to the Bow Valley east of present-day Banff. In doing so they discovered Dolomite Pass (see Dolomite Pass History).

The peak is mentioned in Edwards's book *Trail to the Charmed Land* as "...an attractive-looking mountain of considerable height to which they had given the name of Observation Peak. This mountain did not seem to present any great difficulty, at any rate to experienced mountaineers such as composed our party..." Both parties returned to camp on a warm July evening to share one another's stories of a rather adventurous day.

The first ascent of Observation Peak was actually made some years earlier, in 1895, by Bill Peyto and Walter Wilcox, but they left the mountain unnamed. William Peyto was born in Welling, Kent (now London), on February 14, 1869. "Wild Bill" left England to arrive in Halifax in February 1887, and soon found work as a labourer in Golden, BC, with the CPR. He began working with Tom Wilson as a horse outfitter and guide in the Canadian Rockies in 1893. Peyto amassed a modest collection of books, enabling him to educate himself about geology and paleontology.

Walter Dwight Wilcox was one of Bill Peyto's first clients, hiring him to explore the Bow Lake area and the now nearby Peyto Lake region. Peyto was not fond of climbing mountains, but Wilcox coaxed him into attempting this apparently easy task. After reaching the summit and absorbing the overwhelming scenery, Peyto remarked that he now appreciated the mania for climbing mountains.

Peyto Lake from the false summit of Observation Peak.

Wrapping around a rock band on the scramble to the false summit of Observation Peak.

3. FAIRVIEW MOUNTAIN

Due to its proximity to Chateau Lake Louise, its relative ease and more than fair views, this is one of the most hiked scrambles in the area. Possibly because of these features, this seems to be a gathering place for amateur hikers from all over the world. A true delight. The name, of course, describes the views from this stout mountain. It was, and still is, used as a warm-up climb for mountaineers in the spring while waiting for snow to leave the higher, more "important" mountains. The panorama from the summit is surprisingly amazing for such a short, easy climb, providing proof that sometimes life's small efforts yield great returns.

DIFFICULTY ▲ ▲
ELEVATION GAIN: 1006 M

Trailhead: GPS: N51 24 59.6 W116 12 57.6
Elevation: 1748 m

Fairview Mountain Summit: GPS: N51 23 58.2 W116 13 28.1
Elevation: 2754 m

Trailhead: Drive 5 km up Lake Louise Road from the Lake Louise townsite toward the Chateau. Turn left into the public parking lot just before the private access to the Chateau. The trailhead is signed as "Saddleback Pass" and is on the south shore of Lake Louise toward the boathouse.

The climb is straightforward, as the trail begins by rolling gradually up toward Saddleback Pass. Saddleback Pass is a col between Saddle Mountain and Fairview Mountain that gains 595 m in altitude within 3.7 km. The trail starts in a forest of lodgepole pine and spruce, and within 30–40 minutes emerges from the forest to a more severe grade of switchbacks. The openness of the switchbacks has the benefit of revealing superb views of both mountains. At the approach of the pass and its meadows, Mount Temple looms magnificently to the south (left) and Sheol Mountain directly ahead with a summit elevation of 2780 m.

127

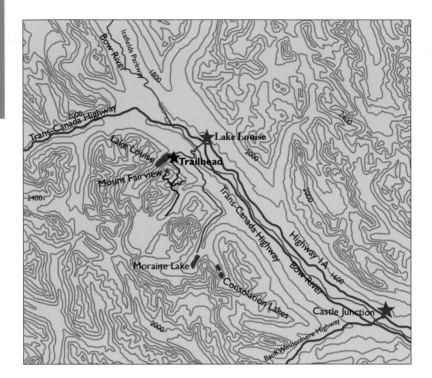

At the apex of Saddleback Pass the trail splits in three directions, going left up Saddle Mountain, straight descending into Paradise Valley and right (northwest) resuming the way to Fairview's summit. There is a sign here marking the correct route. Stop at this pass and enjoy the sights and the international tourists before climbing the remaining 411 m.

The trail cuts back into a small growth of trees, quickly giving way to a steep, rocky slope that begins to wind back and forth up the side of Fairview Mountain. This section is the most laborious part of the outing, as it climbs relentlessly on exposed switchbacks for the last stretch. There is no shame in stopping to catch one's breath, as well as the spectacular scenery, while plodding up this slope of rubble. Too often we feel the urge to accomplish these scrambles in record time or to keep ahead of the group behind us. It is surprising to see how many people turn their wrist to look at their watch while climbing up such mountains. Although awareness of the time of day is necessary to avoid being caught in the dark, try hiking with your watch in your pack instead of on your wrist. It is not a race; go at your own pace.

Soon enough the summit is reached and the reason for the mountain's name becomes clear. Mount Victoria is clearly visible 6.3 km to the southwest and Sheol Mountain 1.8 km directly south. Across the opposite side of Lake Louise are the peaks of Mounts St. Piran and Niblock. The prize on this hike, however, is the outstanding sight of Mount Temple. Avoid the temptation to descend the north face of Fairview Mountain summit, as it becomes steep with narrow ledges and many cliffs. Many day hikers have become trapped here over the years, and sadly one climber was killed in 1992 while going down this shortcut to Lake Louise.

Don Brown hanging out on a ledge on Mount Fairview. Actually, this is an illusion as he is sitting on a wide, flat plateau.

The northward summit view from Mount Fairview.

129

4. MOUNT ST. PIRAN

The quick scramble to the top of Mount St. Piran will only take a few hours, but it is a climb of relentless switchbacks with only a modest number of short, flat spots. Much like Fairview Mountain on the opposite shore of Lake Louise, the trail is absolutely jammed with tourists. The vast majority of them, however, are on their way to the Lake Agnes Teahouse, and they will never even see the summit of the mountain. You are now one of the very few people that veer right instead of left and carry on to the top.

DIFFICULTY ▲
ELEVATION GAIN: 894 M

Trailhead:	GPS: N51 24 59.6 W116 12 57.6
	Elevation: 1748 m
Junction off Beehives Trail:	GPS: N51 25 09.8 W116 14 28.9
	Elevation: 2197 m
Summit:	GPS: N51 25 18.2 W116 15 12.1
	Elevation: 2642 m

Trailhead: Possibly the most popular panorama in the entire Canadian Rockies is the view of Lake Louise in front of the Chateau. Walk on the paved lakeside trail on the right side toward the trail to the Lake Agnes Teahouse. The path to the teahouse and Mirror Lake are amply marked as it quickly jaunts upward to the right, leaving the lakeshore. The trail marker indicates 2.6 km to Mirror Lake at this junction. Less than five minutes later another trail sign shows the way again. After hiking up the trail for about 40 minutes you are joined by the unmistakable marking of a horse trail: the way becomes laden with horse bombs and the accompanying odour.

Mirror Lake is just up the way from this intersection and is an excellent setting to stop, put your feet up and look around. The more than adequate signage directs traffic to Lake Agnes and now the Beehives. Take the right

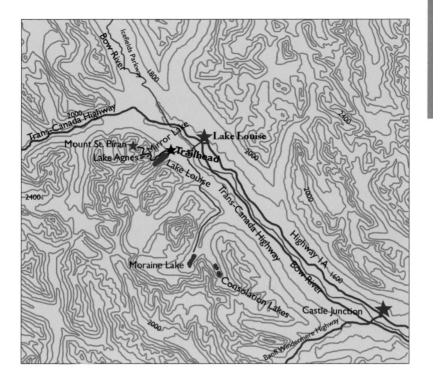

branch of the path, wandering with the pack toward the teahouse. The reason there is such a considerable number of people becomes apparent as the climb progresses: it is absolutely beautiful up here. You have to accept the fact that all of these hundreds of people are here to experience such a wonderfully unique space, just as you are. However, when the signage directs everyone else left to the teahouse and only you go up the trail to the right, you become incredibly aware that your journey is much more significant. So, turn right and walk toward the Beehives. They are 700 m from the fork in the road. However, the marker for Mount St. Piran is located on the left, off the trail, long before you reach the Beehives.

You've now achieved 449 m, with 445 left to go. After you step onto this tributary trail, it slumbers through a forest of spruce for a short time to awaken to the open hillside of the southeast slope of Mount St. Piran. The trail is a combination of compact gravel and scree zigzagging toward the summit. The path steepens as it nears the top, so prepare to expend significant energy just when you think you are there. This open slope lends extraordinary views of Lake Louise and the Chateau.

Fairview Mountain is visible directly across Lake Louise to the southwest. Mount Niblock is almost due west at 252°, 1.4 km away, and Mount Whyte is directly south of that.

History of Fairview Mountain and Mount St. Piran

While spending the summer of 1893 camped on the shores of Lake Louise, Yale student Walter Wilcox and Yale undergraduate Samuel E.S. Allen summited Fairview Mountain. It was later named by Wilcox in 1894, as was Mount St. Piran by Allen. The reason for Fairview's name is obvious, while that of Mount St. Piran is a little more complicated. Coming from Perranuthnoe, Cornwall, England, Willoughby John Astley was the first manager of the Chateau Lake Louise and constructed the first lodge. Prior to that, he had also built the first lodge at Lake Minnewanka. St. Piran is the patron saint of Cornwall.

A fire had levelled the Chateau in 1893, forcing Wilcox and Allen to spend the season in tents. Their return trip to Lake Louise the following year carried grand plans of exploration, photography and mountaineering. Fortunately for them the Chateau Lake Louise had been rebuilt in 1894 just prior to their arrival, allowing them to live in relative comfort. Twelve dollars a week bought them food and lodging and the use of fishing gear, horses and a boat. They were set for the summer.

Their group consisted of three other members as well, forming a club called the Yale Lake Louise Climbing Club. The young men of the club had an extraordinarily busy and productive summer, ending the climbing season by exploring and documenting over 50 square miles of territory around Lake Louise. Their efforts produced the first serious map of the region. All of these accomplishments were achieved without any experience except for a book on mountaineering which they had breezed through only briefly before their craving and enthusiasm to climb overcame them.

The discoveries by Wilcox and Allen during those two summers are astounding. Wilcox wrote about his initial sighting of Moraine Lake:

A friendly golden-mantled ground squirrel was trying to share the author's lunch on the summit of Mount St. Piran.

Mount St. Piran.

Mirror Lake and Lake Louise from the open slope of Mount St. Piran.

The approach to the summit of Mount St. Piran.

133

...no scene has ever given me an equal impression of inspiring solitude and rugged grandeur. I stood on a great stone of the moraine where, from a slight elevation, a magnificent view of the lake lay before me, and while studying the details of this unknown and unvisited spot, spent the happiest half hour of my life.

The lake derived its name from what Wilcox incorrectly thought was the moraine left behind by the Wenkchemna Glacier. What appeared to be a moraine was in fact rubble that had fallen from nearby peaks on the shores of the lake.

Paradise Valley was found while making a second (possibly third) attempt to ascend Mount Lefroy. The Wilcox party were once more on the Lefroy Glacier on a day that was grey and dreary with most of the scenery blocked by cloud, fog and mist. With rain and snow pelting down on them they topped Mitre Pass as the gloom lifted, revealing "... a valley of surpassing beauty, wide and beautiful, with alternating open meadows and rich forests." The "sunlit fairyland" would be named Paradise Valley.

The accidental, surprising discovery of the Valley of the Ten Peaks was possibly the most spectacular find for the Yale Club. The men originally named the ten peaks with Native names, but over the years most were renamed to commemorate explorers and dignitaries.

When all was said and done the five young men had named and/or climbed most of the peaks, glaciers, lakes, passes and valleys in the Lake Louise area. Almost all of the places one visits in and around Lake Louise today were first visited and named by one or more of the Yale Lake Louise Climbing Club. They accomplished all of this with hardly any training, guidance or equipment and more or less did it as they set out on a summer holiday.

5. CINQUEFOIL MOUNTAIN

Cinquefoil Mountain is an exquisite climb through forest, a lakeside stroll, a creek crossing and an ascent through a vast hillside meadow. Views of the Athabasca Valley, including two large, beautiful lakes are plentiful on this scramble and are the main reason for making this trek. The minor reasons are a sense of accomplishment like no other, a great physical workout, fresh air, getting off the couch, peace and tranquility.

DIFFICULTY ▲ ▲ ▲
ELEVATION GAIN: 1240 M

Trailhead:	GPS: N53 03 57.9 W118 03 44.3
	Elevation: 1026 m
Cinquefoil Junction:	GPS: N53 03 52.2 W118 03 13.8
	Elevation: 1036 m
Cinquefoil Summit:	GPS: N53 03 20.2 W117 59 57.6
	Elevation: 2266 m

Trailhead: Drive 26 km east on Highway 16 from the Icefields Parkway traffic lights. There is an unmarked pullover on the south (right) side of the highway where the only amenity is a garbage can. The trailhead is actually the Jacques Creek/Merlin Creek trailhead.

This trail stays level for about 1.5 km, as it begins by heading directly into the forest from the parking lot. Within five minutes a small unnamed lake appears through the trees, and the trail follows the close side of it, continuing eastward (left) as it weaves its way along the lakeshore. Cross the outlet stream over a small bridge and continue through the forest. Depending on the water level of the lake, a small amount of bushwhacking may be necessary to manoeuvre around high water, and the bridge may not be reachable. Beyond the stream, thick brush encroaches upon both sides of the trail until you come to a small clearing. Continue back into

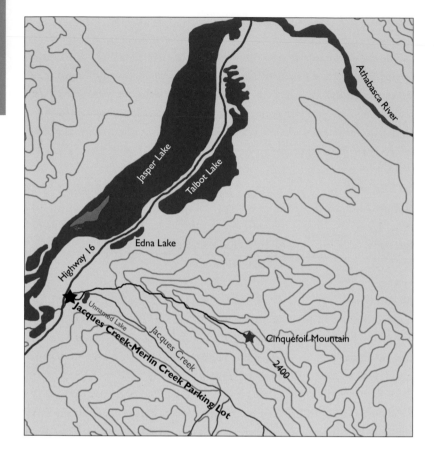

thick bush for a few minutes until reaching another, larger clearing. Here, look for a trail branching off to the left that is well marked with cairns and ribbons (N53 03 52.2 W118 03 13.8). If you miss this intersection, the trail continues straight up the Jacques Creek/Merlin Creek trail. From here the trail re-enters the forest for five to ten minutes before emerging into a large, open hillside meadow.

The now-sparse trail wends its way up the grassland to meld into solid limestone. A multitude of trails split off to go into the forest on the left or the open rock on the right. The preference is an individual one, as the forest route offers easier hiking with little elevation loss but poorer viewing.

Either way, you eventually find yourself on an open scree patch presenting monotonous toil, as all scree does. This eventually breaks through to rubble at the top of a knoll.

Reaching the summit on this slope will seem to be never ending, as you never really see it until you are almost on top of it. A summit ridge, such as this, is a fantastic opportunity to look around, so try to take your attention away from the summit and truly take advantage of what is being offered up here. The summit will be there for eons, while you may never be back to this place again.

Across the Athabasca Valley looking northwest are Mount Greenock, Gargoyle Mountain and Esplanade Mountain almost due west at true bearing 283°. However, the undeniable attraction from here is the view of the Athabasca Valley with Talbot and Jasper lakes to the north.

History

Mount Cinquefoil was named by Morrison Parsons Bridgland in 1916. The name is derived from the flower, which blooms in abundance in the Rocky Mountains. The five-petalled yellow flowers consist of two assortments: the shrubby cinquefoil and the alpine cinquefoil. The shrubby cinquefoil is in full bloom almost all summer long, from early June to early September. These hardy little plants grow anywhere in any summer conditions in the montane to lower subalpine regions. The alpine version blossoms only in the early summer, from early June to mid-July. It is most commonly found in rocky, windy spots.

Born December 20, 1878, in Toronto, Bridgland graduated with honours from the University of Toronto in 1902. Soon after, he became a qualified Dominion land surveyor, and immediately upon his arrival in the West in 1902 he found himself working for A.O. Wheeler as an assistant.

A substantial aspect of Bridgland's surveying technique was photo-topography, for which he became widely respected and admired as a pioneer of the method in the mountain West along with Wheeler and the Surveyor-General of Canada of the day, Édouard-Gaston Deville (1849–1924). One of the fundamental facets of the method was to photo-graph terrain from the highest vantage point in the area being surveyed,

137

so one of the side benefits for Bridgland was that he also became an accomplished mountaineer. He must have become extraordinarily fit as well, given that the work entailed carrying some 35 pounds of equipment up each summit, in addition to the normal climbing gear, which itself was much heavier in those days.

In the off-season, Bridgland would spend his winters in a Calgary office scrutinizing his films in great detail, eventually producing precise topographical maps of the Rockies.

Along with Wheeler, Bridgland became one of the founding members of the Alpine Club of Canada. He mainly organized climbs, but assisted with all outdoor activities for summer camps, keeping meticulous reports of all of these endeavours.

Mount Bridgland in Jasper National Park was named by C.B. Sissons in 1923.

The summit slope of Mount Cinquefoil as seen from a clearing along the trail.

Jasper Lake on the left and Talbot Lake from Mount Cinquefoil.

138

6. MOUNT RUNDLE

This climb deserves all of the accolades it has received. It has tremendous height with great elevation gain and presents the most exposure of any scramble in this book. Additionally, it is the most recognizable peak in the Banff townsite vicinity. But above and beyond all of that, the best thing about Mount Rundle is that no matter where you are in the Banff area you can look up at this huge slab of limestone and proclaim "Hey, I climbed to the top of that mountain!"

DIFFICULTY ▲ ▲ ▲ ▲
ELEVATION GAIN: 1426 M

| Trailhead: | GPS: N51 09 35.6 W116 09 09.0 |
| | Elevation: 1497 m |

| Mount Rundle Summit: | GPS: N51 08 55.9 W115 29 42.3 |
| | Elevation: 2923 m |

Trailhead: Parking for the trailhead is at the Bow Falls parking lot. From the Banff townsite drive across the Bow River Bridge at the south end of Banff Avenue. Turn left onto Spray River Road and drive 750 m to Bow Falls Avenue on the left. Turn down here to the Bow Falls parking lot.

After checking out the falls, walk across the narrow Spray River Bridge. As soon as the bridge is crossed, there is a trail on the right skirting the upper edge of the 15th fairway of the Banff Springs golf course. This trail was made here to cross the course and prevent hikers from running across the middle of the fairway, so be sure to cross here and not farther down. This is the same route taken to the Spray River Loop trailhead. Staying on this trail along the edge of the fairway, now on the other side, will direct you to the Spray River/Mount Rundle signage within a few moments.

The path climbs ever so slightly, levelling off after a moderate gain in elevation. Getting off the Spray River Loop Trail to Mount Rundle is easy, as the trail is well marked right up to its departure to the left. It then begins its slow, monotonous switchback climb through the forest. However, one

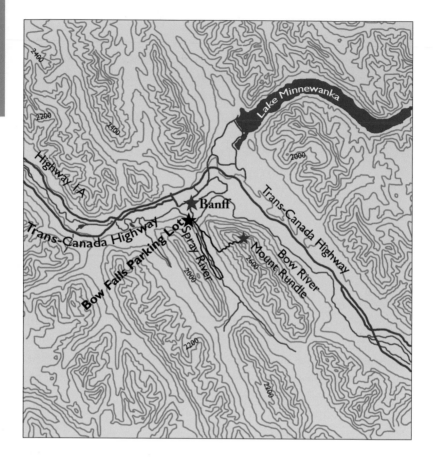

should enjoy the tranquility of this rocky mountain forest, because before long it opens up to the massive limestone slab that is entirely exposed to the elements. Stay on the main trail, avoiding any minor trail diversions to the left, up the slope. These lead to more technical climbs that are rarely used and are beyond mere scrambling techniques.

About halfway up the trail you will encounter a large drainage ditch that may seem irresistible to climb, but please resist. Although the summit is visible from here, this route is full of impassable rock walls. Cross this gully and stick to the course of the well-marked trail. This climb is one of the most frequented in the National Park system, so holding to the trail is straightforward. You will cross this gully and re-enter the forest, onto steeper switchbacks. Once above treeline the footing beneath you becomes unpredictable, as pebbles cover the smooth, slanted limestone. This is an affirmation that proper footwear with sufficient grip is essential.

Soon you will reach a mental barrier known as the Dragon's Back. Although no one has fallen from this obstacle, the danger here is quite real, as either side of this narrow strip has nothing to offer except air and rock. After only a few short minutes, you will have conquered the Dragon's Back, and you will now be faced with an endless, tedious battle with scree and rubble. This truly is the epitome of three steps forward and two steps back. However, don't despair. My mountaineering friend Peter tells me that climbing scree puts him into a trance-like state and that it is a unique method of meditation. It can be very exhilarating if you want it to be. Whether you reach Enlightenment or not, at least the summit is soon within reach. Keep plodding up this rubble, simply taking it one step at a time and eventually the rocky summit is accomplished. Looking directly across the Spray River Valley (west), you'll see Sulphur Mountain, with Sanson Peak at the northern edge of this ridge. On a clear day one can see two Rocky Mountain icons off in the distance: Mount Temple is 54.5 km to the northwest, with a true bearing of 295°, and Mount Assiniboine is 33 km to the south, at 200°.

History

This magnificent, unique mountain was named after Rev. Robert Terrill Rundle (1811–1896) in 1858 by John Palliser. Reverend Rundle was a Methodist missionary to the Indians of the Northwest. He was one of four clergy the Hudson's Bay Company asked to establish missions in their regions. He arrived in Fort Edmonton on October 17, 1840, from England. Rundle was born in Mylor, Cornwall, in 1811 and attended business school in Boscastle in 1837. While in school, he became interested in the Wesleyan Church and was ordained in 1840.

Edmonton became the centre of his territory, allowing him to travel extensively throughout the prairies, the North and into the Rockies. He stayed in Canada for eight years, ultimately returning to England for medical assistance for an injured arm sustained when he fell off his horse in July of 1847. The injury had become persistent due to inadequate medical care and never really healed properly. He left for England in 1848 and never returned.

Rundle travelled with the Indians for years, becoming entranced by both the indigenous peoples and the mountains. He worked so extensively with the Cree, Assiniboine and Métis that he learned to speak Cree, writing hymns for them in their language.

It was James Hector who chose the original name of Terrace Mountain on one of the Palliser expeditions in the area, in 1858. This was short lived, however, as Palliser himself renamed it "Mount Rundle," also in 1858, because of the extraordinary work Rev. Rundle had performed with the Natives.

The first ascent of Mount Rundle was in 1888 by J.J. McArthur while on a surveying assignment in the Bow Valley.

The magnificent, unmistakable limestone face of the southwest slope of Mount Rundle.

Banff townsite from the summit of Mount Rundle looking north.

7. CASTLE MOUNTAIN

The summit of Castle Mountain is an easy, yet lengthy journey. Be prepared for an early morning start and a late afternoon return. There are only two strenuous sections on the trail. The first one is from Tower Lake to Rockbound Lake, and the other is the section from Rockbound Lake to the upper plateau. Otherwise, it is a long meander up 12 km of a moderate incline. With an overall elevation gain approaching 1400 m, more than half of this is accomplished in the 7.7 km to Tower Lake.

The journey to this summit is a trek unlike any other. When you look at this fortress wall from the highway, the summit appears to be almost impossible to achieve beyond this impregnable rock fortification. But the key to this ascent is that the access is actually around the back end of the limestone wall. The journey is truly better than the destination.

DIFFICULTY ▲ ▲ ▲ ▲
ELEVATION GAIN: 1379 M

Trailhead:	GPS: N51 16 08.0 W115 54 57.5
	Elevation: 1396 m
Rockbound Lake:	GPS: N51 18 46.7 W115 55 40.8
	Elevation: 2221 m
Castle Summit:	GPS: N51 18 04.5 W115 55 40.0
	Elevation: 2775 m

Trailhead: The trailhead is located at Castle Junction, 24 km east of Lake Louise on the Trans-Canada Highway. After exiting at the interchange, head north to Highway 1A and proceed east (right) for 200 m. The trail is marked as the "Rockbound Lake" trail, not the "Castle Lookout" trail.

Like many Rocky Mountain scrambles, this route begins in a dense forest. The trail is usually in good repair, with no trouble spots. Carry on up this gentle hike until reaching Tower Lake at kilometre 7.7. Coming out of

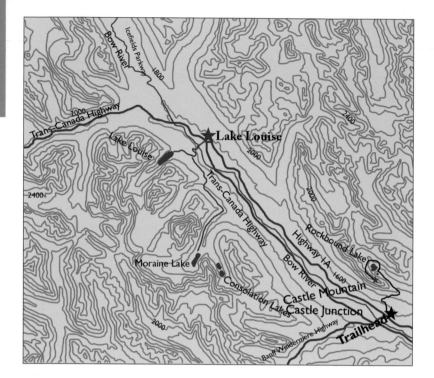

the forest into the meadow before this lake is quite an incredible surprise. Eisenhower Tower looms over the left, as the lake is just in front of you. From here the trail breaks out of the forest into beautiful openness that lets the eyes wander. Because of the design of this climb, you will travel 4.3 km in a wide loop to eventually come back to this approximate point, but 650 m higher.

Follow the trail around the right (northeast) shoreline of Tower Lake to continue up to Rockbound Lake. This is the first heart-thumping part of the climb. There are continual switchbacks straight up through forest, with an elevation gain of very nearly 100 m. It is somewhere up this dirty, dusty section of the trail that you will curse my name. However, it is also the point at which you will wish you had spent the extra time on the treadmill during those long winter nights.

As you come out on the top of this stretch of trail, the unique Rockbound Lake comes into view. Stop and take a breather. Give the old heart a break before attempting to get to the upper plateau. This gorgeous lake is aptly named for the limestone walls surrounding it, with the far shoreline bound by Helena Ridge. Before proceeding up to the plateaus remember to rehydrate, and fill your containers as well. There is still a long way to go and there is no guarantee of water up top. The rock of the eastern main ranges of this area lies flatter than in the more eastern front range mountains. Consequently, they lack the trench-like drainage of the front range peaks, causing the drainage to spread unevenly, and consequently it is not pooled for a long time.

Follow the shoreline to the right, travelling north, until you reach the drainage outflow of the lake. Cross this small stream and continue heading toward the gullies straight ahead. Pick up the trail here that will arrive at the furthest channel on the right. Climb up this gully to embark on the second strenuous part of the trek. This ravine trail is well trodden and maintains its course right up to the upper plateau.

As you emerge from the gully into a small clearing, the summit comes into view behind you. It is almost as far back as can be seen, to the southeast with a bearing of 172° true, 1.9 km distant as the crow flies. As the hiker treks, however, the long ridge walk to the summit is indeed 3 km, with only a slight elevation gain of 356 m. Once you are up and out of this gorge, the remainder of the route becomes a choice between two routes. The recommended time-saving route is to take the low left trail and not the steep climb up to the right. The low trail will descend onto a vast grassy area, which has a lovely clear stream carved through it. At the far end of the grass plateau look for a cairn-marked gully. This is a quick climb back up to the upper terrace. Alternatively, after climbing up from Rockbound Lake, stay to the right, up a steep knoll. The traverse on the upper terrace is longer than the shortcut through the grassy table, but is actually a less complicated approach. Regardless, both routes converge at the upper terrace trail toward the summit. The remainder of the hike consists of a lot of rock hopping on rubble. This first appears to be never ending and becomes rather laborious as you hop on rock after rock after rock. However, as the rock hopping persists, it becomes evident that elevation is being gained without the tedium of a direct route upward. Off in the distance the summit is visible as a rocky outcrop. Clamber to the top of this to reach the exposed summit of Castle Mountain.

The summit is a natural viewpoint with such sights as Pilot Mountain 14.4 km to the southeast and Mount Temple 20 km off to the west. Directly below are the Trans-Canada Highway and the Castle Junction Interchange, a reminder of how far you have come today.

History

This rugged fortress of a mountain was first named because of its obvious appearance, by James Hector of the Palliser Expedition, on August 17, 1858. Dr. Hector had been sent to explore the Bow Valley and search for the source of the Bow River. He was guided by a Stoney guide, Nimrod, who drew a map of the route that Hector should take to find his objective. The map, incidentally, put Hector and his crew on an indirect course, finally coming out of Vermilion Pass, which is today's Banff-Windermere Highway. He spotted the mountain from a distance of 12 miles, remarking that it "... looks exactly like a gigantic castle," and named it on the spot.

On January 9, 1946, however, the name was changed to Mount Eisenhower to commemorate a visit by the commander of the allied forces in Europe during the Second World War. That name stuck for 33 years until 1979, when Castle Mountain regained its rightful identity, leaving only the singular southeast pillar of the massif, Eisenhower Tower, named for the US general and president.

In 1883 as rumours of gold, silver and copper in the area spread, Silver City, near Castle Mountain, erupted into a town of over 3,000 inhabitants. John Gerome Healy had a hand in the formation of the town, as he had done some mining at nearby Copper Mountain and had experience building towns, notably forts Whoop-up and Hamilton. These profitable forts were used for the sole purpose of trading whisky to the Natives for buffalo robes.

Healy actually named the town "Copper Mine" but the railway had its own way of doing things and named the stop "Silver City." The glory was short lived, however, as the five or so mines did not produce any significant profit. There was an unconfirmed report of silver being imported from Montana and planted around Castle Mountain to maintain the excitement and keep the miners in the neighbourhood. Regardless of the efforts, Silver City became a ghost town within two years.

The back end of Castle Mountain as seen from the Trans-Canada Highway. The route is easily recognized.

The upper plateau of the Castle Mountain journey is finally reached.

Rockbound Lake is one of many highlights along the way to the summit of Castle Mountain.

8. MOUNT BOURGEAU

This adventure has it all: beautiful lakes, waterfalls, streams, a walk through the forest, mountain sheep, spectacular backdrops of mountains and meadows, and a radio repeater station at the summit. This is truly a wonderful journey with a sensational destination.

DIFFICULTY ▲
ELEVATION GAIN: 1463 M

Trailhead:	GPS: N51 08 13.3 W115 47 20.1
	Elevation: 1463 m
Bourgeau Lake:	GPS: N51 08 13.3 W115 47 20.1
	Elevation: 2130 m
Bourgeau Summit:	GPS: N51 07 59.1 W115 46 30.9
	Elevation: 2926 m

Trailhead: Heading west from Banff on Highway 1, drive past the Sunshine turnoff and keep a sharp eye out for the Bourgeau Lake Trail parking lot. It is about 3 km past the Sunshine ski overpass on the left (south) side of the highway.

Walk through a gated fence into the forest and begin to climb gently up switchbacks for 60 to 90 minutes until you reach a clearing with a beautiful waterfall on the left side of the trail. Cross this stream and continue up the trail. Some 7.5 km from the trailhead the sparkling, hypnotic, clear waters of Bourgeau Lake come into view. The shimmering waters of the lake can charm hikers and hold them here for hours. This is an extraordinary place to gaze into the transparent depths and clear one's mind.

After the spell has been broken, follow the path and wander around the right side of the lake upward for a short bit to a subalpine cirque containing two unnamed tarns. Walk farther up the trail by the side of a stream to come upon Harvey Lake in the pass of the same name. As you travel along the

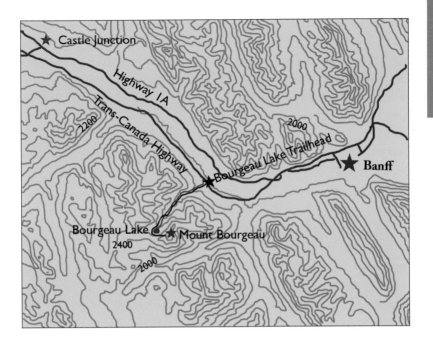

pass there is a knoll on the left (northeast) where mountain sheep frequent the summer growth of grass and flowers. From the pass, the trail stays the course and climbs gradually up another 400 m to the broad summit.

Notable sights from here include Mount Assiniboine south at 163° and over 30 km away; Healy Pass and Meadows just down the hill to the southwest; and Mount Ball almost due west.

History

J.J. McArthur and Tom Wilson were the first to ascend Bourgeau, in 1890. Dr. James Hector had named the peak after Eugène Bourgeau on August 17, 1858. Eugène Bourgeau (1813–1877) was a botanist from Brizon in the French Alps, and his love affair with wildflowers there made him a leading candidate to be the botanist with the Palliser Expedition into the Canadian Rockies. John Palliser's trek became a "scientific" venture to enable the granting of Royal Geographic funding, and to find information about southern passes in the Rocky Mountains.

Hector and Bourgeau began separate expeditions into the valley of the Bow River on the same day, as both had been given directives from the Palliser Expedition. Hector's mission was to find the source of the Bow River and a possible pass to the Columbia River in British Columbia. Bourgeau, on the other hand, was assigned to explore and to collect botanical specimens.

The two parties departed together from Old Bow Fort, near present-day Morley, Alberta, on August 11, 1858, and Hector and Bourgeau became instant friends. The following day the two groups were to go their separate ways, but before parting the pair spent the morning on the slopes of Grotto Mountain, but into the afternoon Bourgeau lingered in the nearby slopes and meadows in the area while Hector pressed on in search of the headwaters of the Bow. Hector noted that "Little Bourgeau" rarely ceased working. He was always busy taking notes, making drawings, studying plants and collecting samples. During this brief time they spent together, Hector was so impressed by Bourgeau's non-stop work ethic that he named a mountain after him. "Looking up the valley to the W.S.W., we had before us a truncated mountain evidently composed of massive horizontal strata and which I named Mount Bourgeau."

The 44-year-old Bourgeau became renowned not only for his work, but also for his cheery, upbeat personality, making him a pleasure to travel with. Palliser wrote, for example, that

> ... [he] has been a most active, energetic and excellent companion, always hard at his work in which his whole soul seems engrossed, and no matter what his fatigues or privations may be, his botanical specimens are always his first care.... Little Bourgeau is a brick, his collections to me (who knows nothing of Botany) very pretty and the colours as vivid after the specimens are saved as they are in life. He is most indefatigable and always at work.

Mount Bourgeau and Lake from Harvey Pass.

A dazzling waterfall that is crossed on the way to Mount Bourgeau.

The vastness of Healy Pass is evident from the approach to the Mount Bourgeau summit.

151

9. CIRQUE PEAK

With a trip to the base of Cirque Peak, the hiker experiences a forest of pine and spruce, alpine meadows, small alpine lakes and charming runoff streams. I cannot imagine a better place to spend a day. Because of the beauty and the variety of activities, such as lake walks, pass summiting, meadow walking and peak bagging, this trail is usually fairly busy. Although I had joined this trail to summit Cirque Peak, one fellow scrambler admitted he had decided he would not summit on that particular day so he would have an excuse to return. He decided to spend the day exploring the meadows and lakes instead.

DIFFICULTY ▲ ▲ ▲
ELEVATION GAIN: 1016

Trailhead:	GPS: N51 39 50.0 W116 26 17.8
	Elevation: 1981 m
Dolomite Pass:	GPS: N51 41 23.4 W116 24 35.1
	Elevation: 2522 m
Cirque Peak Summit:	GPS: N51 42 00.7 W116 25 03.9
	Elevation: 2997 m

Trailhead: Drive north on the Icefields Parkway for 33.8 km from where it intersects with the Trans-Canada Highway 2 km west of Lake Louise. Watch for the Lake Helen parking lot on the right side of the Parkway.

For the first hour most of the trail has exposed roots, making the initial trek appreciably treacherous in wet conditions. Even in dry conditions, exposed roots present an additional hazard of twisting ankles and snapping tendons. The hike is more or less flat for the first 20 to 30 minutes, but then begins to climb, with the forest becoming tighter and limiting scenery to not much of anything other than the forest itself. However, 15 to 20 minutes later the trees begin to thin, allowing sporadic openings to see across the highway to the Waputik Range on the other side of the valley.

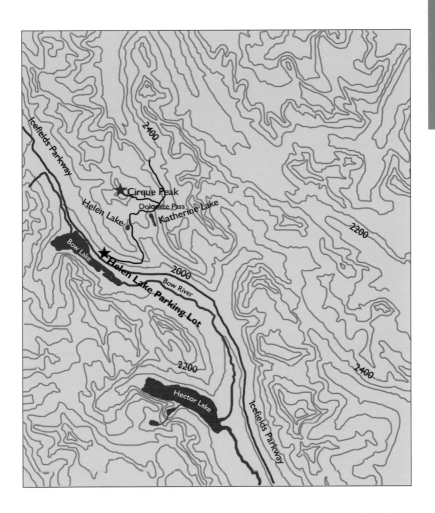

Finally, after you've been hiking for approximately an hour, the forest vanishes, yielding vistas of Dolomite Peak directly ahead and Cirque Peak to the left. The remainder of the trek to Lake Helen is through an alpine meadow, with Cirque Peak dead ahead in the line of sight until you reach the lake. Lake Helen is more of a large pond amidst this alpine meadow, but even so, it is a tranquil spot to stop and look around before hustling up to Dolomite Pass. The trail winds around the east side of the lake and suddenly takes up with the hillside leading to the summit of Dolomite

Pass. The brief increase in elevation is achieved more quickly by staying to the left at the first trail junction (GPS: N51 41 20.1 W116 24 36.0), partway up the hillside. Within a few quick minutes, Dolomite Pass is conquered.

The way to the Cirque Peak summit is evident, as climbing the exposed east shale shoulder onto the ridge is obvious and should take only one to one and a half hours. There is a small amount of scree and shale, but nothing substantial. For the most part, it is a straightforward walk up the side of the mountain to the ridge and onto the summit. The scenery from the top is unique, allowing a superior view of the Wapta Icefield to the southwest. Observation Peak is a mere 5.2 km away to the northwest.

History

In July of 1899 guide Ralph Edwards was engaged to take four explorers over the Pipestone Pass, down the Siffleur River to the Saskatchewan, up to Bear Creek (today called the Mistaya River) and then up to Bow Lake. The purpose of the expedition was to do some climbing and adventuring around the Bow Lake area. The party consisted of two lawyers, George Weed and Charles S. Thompson, and two clergymen, C.L. Noyes and Harry P. Nicholls. Of these four men, Edwards wrote:

> There is an old saying used to describe a person of outstanding character that when 'God made him He broke the mould,' thus signifying that there were no others quite his equal; if this be so, in the present instance He broke four moulds.

After several days on the trail, the group found themselves "... between the valley of the Pipestone and the Bow." What they did not know was where they were going to come out. One evening near Bow Lake, after supper, Edwards suggested that the following day the group should stay camped there and do some climbing while he would set out to find a shortcut to the Bow Valley somewhere north of Hector Lake. Edwards and Weed departed early the following morning, while the rest of the group climbed a nearby mountain and subsequently named it Observation Peak.

After facing a rockslide, which required clambering over, and then what looked like a box canyon to navigate, Edwards finally spotted a gap in the valley they were exploring. The gap went up a gentle slope for perhaps 150 feet. Behind it there were no mountains, and from their vantage point it appeared to flatten out. They had discovered what they had set out in search of. According to Edwards's book *Trail to the Charmed Land,* "The pass was actually a beautiful, almost level alpine meadow, and to our left lay a lovely blue lake nestled at the base of the steep cliffs which terminated the eastern range." The following evening, when the entire group camped at Lake Katherine, there was no wood for a fire, no sign of previous fires and not even a single teepee pole in sight. Edwards and Weed were quite certain they were the first humans ever to cross this pass.

Dolomite Pass got its name because of their similarity to the formations of the Dolomites of Italy. Lakes Katherine and Helen are named for the daughters of Rev. Nichols. Cirque Peak, named much later, in 1909, is so called simply because there is a large cirque at the base of the cliff.

Cirque Peak from Dolomite Pass.

Lake Helen and meadows from Dolomite Pass.

10. MOUNT WILCOX

The first hour of this hike is a journey that has its own distinctive scenery as the trail winds upward on a hillside devoid of any obstacles. There is so much to see on the way toward the base of the mountain that the hour and a half walk goes by very quickly. The Athabasca Glacier, the Columbia Icefield Centre and Mounts Kitchener and Andromeda are but a few of the vast sights which overload the hiker here. Mount Wilcox and Nigel Peak are both accessed from Wilcox Pass, and the two of them have two well-defined summit tracks.

DIFFICULTY ▲ ▲ ▲
ELEVATION GAIN: 863 M

Trailhead: GPS: N52 13 05.5 W117 11 04.9
                            Elevation: 2018 m

Mount Wilcox Summit: GPS: N52 14 39.0 W117 14 28.5
                            Elevation: 2881 m

Trailhead: The trailhead for Wilcox Pass is at the lower parking lot of Wilcox Creek Campground, on the east side of the Icefields Parkway 2.8 km south of the Columbia Icefield Centre, or 127 km north of the junction of the Trans-Canada Highway and the Icefields Parkway. Follow the trailhead marker for Wilcox Pass.

The initial walk toward Mount Wilcox takes the same path as the hike toward Nigel Peak. They both loom over Wilcox Pass, making it possible to bag two peaks in one day. Unfortunately, overnight camping is not permitted in Wilcox Pass. The trail heads into a forest of tall, thin pines with scattered firs and begins to climb directly from the parking lot. As the elevation increases, the forest thins out and within ten minutes allows proportionately finer views to the west of the Winston Churchill Range that is home to the Columbia Icefield. Ten more minutes of easy climbing through a forest of subalpine firs places the trail on a hillside of complete exposure, giving even grander sights as the worn path

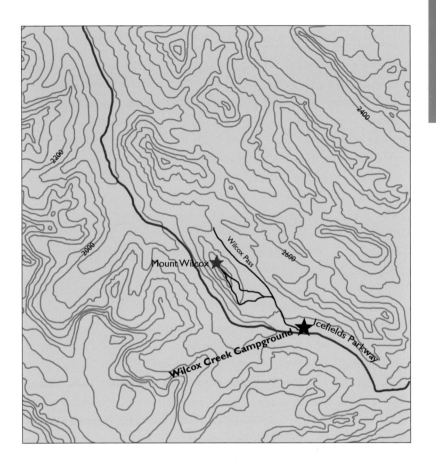

ascends toward Wilcox Pass. Twenty more minutes of intoxicating uphill walking and the trail levels off at Wilcox Pass.

Continue along the main trail and after an hour or more from the trailhead an elevated, marked viewpoint is unmistakable on the right side of the path. Some 15–20 m past the marker, the trail toward Mount Wilcox takes a left turn off the main corridor. As mentioned, there are two routes up Mount Wilcox and they both begin at this intersection. Regardless of which path you take, there is only 531 m left to scramble, as most of the elevation has been achieved while hiking up to Wilcox Pass. Of the two approaches, the obvious one is on the east slope, where the trail is very visible as you close in on the mountain. The other way begins at the foot of the mountain on the far south end of it.

It takes about ten additional minutes to get to the base of the mountain doing the south option, but it is a much easier journey walking up a gradual incline atop a gorgeous ridge. After turning onto the left trail, heading west, continue on this for 30 minutes, making certain you skirt around the left side of the massive bog you may be tempted to shortcut across. The views from the ridge walk allow for grander sights, since both the east and west sides of the mountain can be accessed. The only obstacle that breaks up the walk is a rock wall another 20 minutes into the hike. Really, this only appears to be an obstacle; by following the trail right to the rock, you'll find a crack in the wall that allows easy access up to the top. Once you are up there, continue the trail until it converges with the ridge to reach the east trail.

The rubble path meandering up the east slope is visible from the viewpoint intersection and is the most popular way. Follow the same trail as the first route, turning left just beyond the viewpoint, but veer off it and over the open alpine sooner rather than later. There does not appear to be a defined trail across the meadows, so try to avoid stomping on the foliage and set foot on firm ground whenever possible. Even though the path up the side of the east slope has been beaten down, it still consists of rubble and scree, making this choice somewhat more laborious. Supplement this with a steeper, more direct challenge with fewer views, and the southern option is definitely preferred.

Regardless of which course you take, they both join atop a beautiful plateau. The stroll on the plateau allows for lung, heart and leg recovery while enjoying the scenery. This ends shortly, though, as you approach a large rock abutment that is impenetrable. There is a trail leading to the bluff, as many scramblers have vainly attempted to conquer it. Watch for the path that stays level and bypasses the bluff on the scree slope around the right side of it. Since this is a scree slope, many trails fade and then reappear, but they are there, so stay up high as you traverse the slope, keeping an eye out for cairns and trails. Continue this course until reaching the second bluff, which comes into sight soon after you've circumnavigated the first one. All of the scree trails eventually reach up toward the apex of the second bluff, as they all converge at a notch near the top. From here, overtaking the bluff is easy.

This has been a lot of work so far, but the summit is now within reach. Popping up out of the notch, you immediately see the summit, and a five- to ten-minute walk on terra firma puts you there. Congratulations. The true summit involves some moderate exposure (see p. 166 as to "exposure").

Views are 360 degrees, displaying Nigel Peak almost due east at 96° true, Mount Athabasca to the southeast and Snow Dome 8 km to the southeast.

Mount Athabasca seems close enough to touch from the summit of Mount Wilcox.

The braided entanglement of the Athabasca River from the Mount Wilcox Summit. Use caution while gazing from the summit of Mount Wilcox. The drop is immense.

11. NIGEL PEAK

The hike to the base of Nigel Peak is an absolute wonder on its own. The trail to Wilcox Pass is exposed to the hillside overlooking the Icefields Parkway, the Columbia Icefield Centre, the Athabasca and Dome glaciers and a variety of peaks. Like Mount Wilcox on the opposite side of Wilcox Pass, Nigel Peak has two distinct routes for reaching the summit. Depending on the choice, Nigel Peak is either a straight upward, aggravating scree scramble or an exposed ridge walk.

DIFFICULTY ▲ ▲ ▲ ▲ ▲

ELEVATION GAIN: 1182 M

Trailhead:	GPS: N52 13 05.5 W117 11 04.9
	Elevation: 2018 m
Nigel Peak Summit:	GPS: N52 14 21.3 W117 10 19.0
	Elevation: 3200 m

Trailhead: The trailhead is at the parking lot immediately off the highway entering Wilcox Pass Campground and is marked as Wilcox Pass. This parking area is 127 km north of the junction of the Trans-Canada Highway and the Icefields Parkway, on the east side of the Parkway. About 3 km north of this parking lot is the Columbia Icefield Centre.

The initial work toward Nigel Peak takes the same path as the hike toward Mount Wilcox. They both loom over Wilcox Pass, making it possible to bag two peaks in one day. Unfortunately, camping is not permitted in Wilcox Pass. The trail heads into a forest of tall, thin pine trees, with scattered firs and begins to climb directly from the parking lot. As the elevation increases, the forest thins out and within ten minutes allows proportionately finer views westward toward the Winston Churchill Range, which is home to the Columbia Icefield. Ten more minutes of easy climbing through a forest of subalpine firs places you on a hillside of complete exposure, giving you to even grander sights

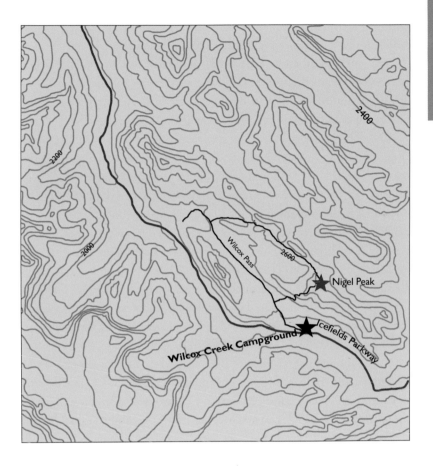

as the worn path ascends toward Wilcox Pass. Twenty more minutes of intoxicating uphill walking sees the trail level off at Wilcox Pass.

As you level out into Wilcox Pass, the summit of Nigel Peak comes into view to the northeast (right) and the 2-km summit ridge dominates the skyline. There are two possible routes to the summit, with the closest one being a tedious vertical drudge of scree and fist-sized rocks. To get to this obvious scree slope, begin crossing over the wide expanse of Wilcox Pass to the visible perpendicular trail to the left of the main peak. As you come closer to this trail, you will understand why such a short climb can consume so much energy, as there is no break in the straight-up ascent until you arrive at the sub-summit ridge crest. At the top of the crest, a saddle lies between the summit ridge and the true peak.

Stay to the right around the saddle and eventually steer left at a rock headwall to attain the south side of the north ridge to the summit. This is actually quite straightforward once you are up there, but there is some modest amount of exposure, so do not take this lightly.

Every single person has his or her own comfort level with "exposure." In scrambling and mountaineering, this term refers not to being out in the open and vulnerable to the elements, but to how precarious a ridgetop or ledge or other footing may be, and thus how much danger there is that an incautious hiker or climber could fall a very long way down. These factors, combined with your overall level of exhaustion during a particular climb, determine each person's comfort zone. When I scramble with my crew, we have a rule that states that if someone does not feel comfortable about a climb, then all of us will turn around and stop for the day, no questions asked. I advise establishing such guidelines before an ascent, to avoid confusion, anger and an undeserved sense of shame during the climb.

The second route is lengthier, but lacks the pain and suffering that a straight-up scree climb has to offer. Instead of cutting directly across Wilcox Pass to the base of the ridge, make a beeline for the much lower, northwest end of the range. At the far end, two well-worn paths venture up to the scree line. Reaching the upper trail is the ultimate goal, and at this spot the trail traverses the scree in a steady incline, making the climb much less intense. Additionally, the elevation gain at this end is far less than the first option, putting you on the summit ridge sooner. The drawback is the extra distance across the pass to the far end of the base of the mountain, as well as the long climb up the 2 km along the summit ridge.

Follow the upper trail up to a small cairn-marked col, and immediately turn right and look over your right shoulder. The sight of a seemingly impenetrable rock wall is somewhat daunting. However, there are three easy ways to overcome this pinnacle by going around to the left, the right or straight up the middle. The most popular route with the least exposure is the path wrapping itself around the left side. Once on top of this obstacle, continue up the summit ridge for a long, spectacular journey toward the summit. The ridge narrows as it progresses to the summit, and your comfort zone may narrow as well. Because of this, you must feel comfortable with the prospect that you may not make the summit and may have to settle for a spectacular ridge walk. Nonetheless, the view from here is still monumental and no less spectacular than the summit. The jaunt here on this route has already delivered great variety and viewing opportunities, and time is just as well spent looking around instead of staring up a scree slope.

Nigel Peak in the foreground from Mount Wilcox.

Looking south down Wilcox Pass between Nigel Peak and Mount Wilcox.

History of Mount Wilcox and Nigel Peak

Walter D. Wilcox discovered Wilcox Pass and the neighbouring Mount Wilcox in 1896 but did not name them. Wilcox was an explorer from the US who set out in 1896 to investigate the headwaters of the Saskatchewan River. The pass became the main link between the Saskatchewan and Athabasca rivers. In 1896 there was not much information or exploration of the region north of Bow Pass, as maps were vague and trails were unknown. Therefore, Wilcox took it upon himself to explore this vast uncharted part of the planet with hopes of making important findings. Among them were Wilcox Pass, Mount Athabasca and the Sunwapta Valley. He only narrowly missed the Columbia Icefield. Quite an outing.

In 1898 mountaineering guide Bill Peyto, with his packer and cook Nigel Vavasour, guided Brits Hugh E.M. Stutfield, Dr. J. Norman Collie and Herman Woolley into this pass, which resulted in the discovery of the Columbia Icefield. Collie named the pass and mountain after Walter Wilcox for his efforts in discovering the pass. The wealth of large game in the area was also of tremendous interest to Peyto and his boss, Tom Wilson, as they had many British and American clients with an appetite for big-game hunting.

Vavasour was involved in many hunts, including sheep, during the expedition, exhibiting considerable skill and perseverance. Collie named Nigel Peak in the course of this journey, but it was not until 1919 that it was summited by members of the Interprovincial Boundary Commission.

A student at Yale University, Wilcox had ventured to the shores of Lake Louise in the summer of 1893 and camped out for the summer, since the original, rustic CPR chateau had burned down that same year. During this summer, Wilcox met Samuel Allen and the two began climbing the mountains in the vicinity. They were the first to summit, and hence name, Fairview Mountain, and made unsuccessful attempts on Mounts Victoria and Temple.

They returned the following summer more focused, better prepared and more determined. They also enjoyed better base-camp comfort than the previous year, as upon their arrival a new Chateau Lake Louise was nearing completion, enabling them to obtain lodging, meals, horses and even a boat for $12 a week. The gentlemen made first ascents of Temple and Aberdeen in 1884 and others, including Niblock and Indefatigable, some years later.

12. MOUNT TEMPLE

Even though the scramble to the summit of Mount Temple involves a short hand-over-hand climb, it is an extensive yet easy scramble to the summit of this highest of the peaks in this guidebook. The only reason it is included, and consequently exposing you to a bit of risk, is because of the absolute euphoria of being at such high altitude. Temple is the third-highest peak in the southern Rockies, the highest in the Lake Louise area, and overall the 11th-highest in the Canadian Rockies. There is much to be said for being so high up that you are looking down on the top of every other mountain in sight. A climbing helmet is recommended for the rock wall.

DIFFICULTY ▲ ▲ ▲ ▲ ▲
ELEVATION GAIN: 1675

Trailhead:	GPS: N51 19 43.3 W116 10 54.0
	Elevation: 1873 m
Sentinel Pass:	GPS: N51 20 26.0 W116 13 18.6
	Elevation: 2619 m
Summit:	GPS: N51 21 03.7 W116 12 23.0
	Elevation: 3548 m

Trailhead: From the town of Lake Louise, drive up Lake Louise Drive toward the Chateau and turn left on Moraine Lake Road. Continue to the Moraine Lake parking lot, approximately 12 km from the turnoff. Hike the right side of the lake, starting behind the Chateau, until you reach Larch Valley Trail.

The 6-km walk to Sentinel Pass covers an ascent via switchbacks through forest, subalpine and alpine regions while passing lakes and streams. Initially, the trail is an hour of relentless switchbacks, finally levelling off to a picturesque walk through the meadows of Larch Valley toward the base of Sentinel Pass. Crossing the meadows should take 20

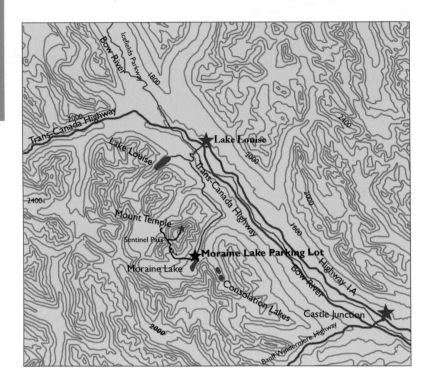

to 30 minutes, allowing your body to rejuvenate before pushing on to the summit. The lower of the Minnestimma lakes is nestled five minutes off the trail to the right, while the upper, larger one is farther up the trail on the left. This is the last source of water before the summit, and it is advisable to filter, as the water in these lakes is still.

The apex of Sentinel Pass is in sight long before you reach it, and the long, arduous switchbacks become visible as you get closer. The Sentinel Pass crest has gained you 746 m, leaving 929 m left to climb. It is here that you may concede there is too much more work to do, but if you wish to feel pure jubilation and triumph, and see what very few people on the planet have seen, then pick up and carry on. This is an experience like no other in your life.

The path courses up the southwest slope on scree trails marked by too many cairns for about a half hour until it comes to the only intimidating part of the entire trip. You should wear a helmet here, as there is loose rock all around. Whether a hiker is going up or coming down, the risk of someone dislodging a rock on your head is very real. When you arrive at an impasse that is about 10 to 15 m high, there are two possible approaches. The first one is a clearly visible hand-over-hand climb up a well-worn route that is easier than it looks. It is a good idea to take a length of rope on this trip to haul your daypacks up and down this bluff. The second option is a narrow crack in the left side of the wall, which has far less exposure but is tricky to find and harder to climb.

From here on up, for the next hour and a half, the route is a remarkable network of trails and switchbacks offering the grandest of views as you weave up the side of the mountain to the large summit. Breathing becomes markedly difficult because the air thins out, making the summit push somewhat longer and more laborious than it appears.

From here, the views are astounding as you look down on everything around you. To the southwest are Hungabee Mountain and Wenkchemna Peak with Horseshoe Glacier and Horseshoe Lake at the base of them. You can see forever from up here.

History

Walter Wilcox, with Samuel Allen and L.F. Frissell, first summited Mount Temple in 1894. In early August, they departed the Lake Louise Chalet with fellow climbers George Warrington and Yandell Henderson and a Stoney Indian named Enoch Wildman to camp in and explore the wilderness of Paradise Valley. They enjoyed a couple of days of climbing and investigating this territory, and on August 17 Wilcox, Allen and Frissell decided to attempt the first ascent of Mount Temple.

The peak had been named ten years earlier by George Mercer Dawson (1849–1901), a geologist, anthropologist, author, teacher, civil servant, geographer and paleontologist. Dawson was born in Nova Scotia and schooled at McGill College in Montreal, the Royal School of Mines in London and the Geological Survey of Great Britain. He published a considerable body of influential scientific work. It was in 1884, when Dawson first came to the Rockies as leader of the British Association for the Advancement of Science Team, that he discovered Mount Temple. He named the peak for Sir Richard Temple (1826–1902), who, after a notable career in India, in particular as Governor of Bombay, returned to England and held numerous public offices, including as Conservative MP and as Privy Councillor.

Mount Temple. Push to the Summit.

The last light of the day embraces Mount Temple. Viewed from the Lake Louise village.

13. TANGLE RIDGE

*Tangle Ridge, as the name implies, is a ridge with a high point classi-
fied as a summit. The ridge makes this scramble a standout, enabling
hikers to stroll to many vantage points offering distinctive views. When
a repeater station sits atop a summit it is usually an eyesore, but on our
last visit it worked as a windbreak when strong winds and sleet caught
us unaware and marooned us there for a couple of hours. This supports
the claim that packing proper rain gear on a hot summer day is necessary, as we were able to stay warm and dry by donning the appropriate
clothing. Even without the protection of the repeater station, we would
have been fine.*

DIFFICULTY ▲ ▲ ▲ ▲
ELEVATION GAIN: 1158 M

Trailhead:	GPS: N52 16 00.9 W117 17 09.5 Elevation: 1847 m
Tangle Creek Cairn:	GPS: N52 16 15.1 W117 16 42.7
Tangle Ridge Summit:	GPS: N52 17 54.1 W117 17 13.8 Elevation: 3005 m

Trailhead: The parking lot for Tangle Falls sits on the west side of the
Icefields Parkway 127 km north of the Parkway/Trans-Canada Highway
junction, 7 km north of the Columbia Icefield Centre and 103 km south
of Jasper. The trailhead is across the highway on the east side, just south of
the falls. A sign directing hikers to Wilcox Pass and Wilcox Campground
puts scramblers on the correct path.

The trail begins as a gentle climb for 20 to 25 minutes, skirting the
Parkway for about 500–600 m, then darting into the bush. The forest of
larch and lodgepole pine is moderately thin but still does not really permit
any notable viewing. It is a single-track trail, mainly used to loop around

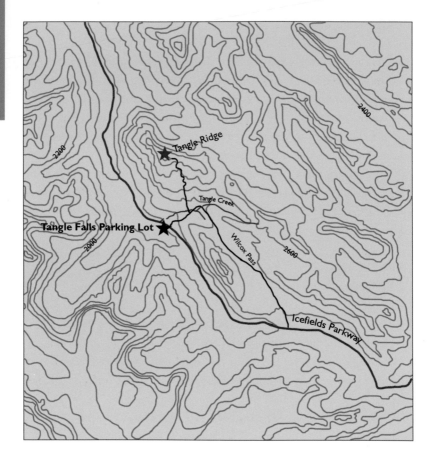

to Wilcox Pass. If, while hiking Wilcox Pass, you have ever wondered where the trail ends, this is the answer.

The trail levels off briefly and begins to descend to meet Tangle Creek. When the path comes close to the creek, begin searching for a faint trail going down to the creekbed. After finding the offshoot path, it is imperative to locate a large, metre-tall cairn up on the bank on the opposite side of the creek. Before crossing, line up Tangle Ridge with the distinctively large cairn and the usually dry gully in which the cairn sits. This gully will take you to the base of Tangle Ridge.

After stone stepping across the creek, search out more cairns farther up the drainage gully. These direct traffic to the right side of the gulch, but trails are faint and not well marked. Nonetheless, pursuing the ditch is easy, and soon enough it enters forest yet again to begin ascending toward the summit. In due course the treeline is attained and the hillside opens up to small pastures on the way to a scree slope. As scree goes, this is not too bad. There is a good trail that seems to have been used extensively, making the usually insufferable scree almost tolerable.

As expected, the sights from the ridge walk are astounding. As you gaze to the southeast, Mount Wilcox and Nigel Peak are visible. Looking northwest down on the Icefields Parkway, you'll see glaciers, rivers, turquoise lakes and more snow-covered peaks as far away as Jasper. Sunwapta Peak is 8° north, 5.8 km away. This peak stands 3320 m above sea level, putting it at almost 11,000 (10,892) feet high.

History

The name "Tangle" is self-explanatory. It comes from Mary Schäffer in a 1907 reference to the difficulty an exploring party had navigating the creek and surrounding forest. The party was coming down from Wilcox Pass, with the Sunwapta River as their destination. Schäffer had complained that the creek and the valley it is situated in was a tangle of trees, deadfall, scrub and impenetrable undergrowth. Another source says the name is derived from the tangled appearance of nearby Sunwapta River.

The long, flat Tangle Ridge from the Icefields Parkway.

14. HA LING PEAK

An easy ascent without any difficulties and no exposure, Ha Ling Peak generates a remarkably exhilarating day. The ascent of 808 m is straightforward and offers terrific panoramas of Mount Rundle and the Goat Range. This is why Ha Ling is a popular destination in the Canmore area, and therefore an early morning start is advised to avoid the significant number of hikers who enjoy this scramble.

DIFFICULTY ▲ ▲ ▲
ELEVATION GAIN: 808 M

Trailhead: GPS: N51 03 42.5 W115 25 06.2
                        Elevation: 1671 m

Ha Ling Summit: GPS: N51 03 50.9 W115 23 57.7
                        Elevation: 2479 m

Trailhead: Whether driving east or west on the Trans-Canada Highway outside of Canmore, simply follow the signs to the Nordic Centre. The directions will take you right through the middle of downtown. Drive past the Nordic Centre on Spray Lakes Road for 1 km. The road turns to gravel and an additional 4.2 km will bring you to the Goat Creek parking lot.

The trailhead is on the opposite side of the road from the parking lot, up an embankment and behind a utility shed beyond a short bridge. The single-track path immediately begins climbing over exposed roots and rocks. Be careful. Fifteen minutes later the grade increases briefly as it passes a foliated drainage ravine on the right side of the trail. Soon afterward, the trail loses the exposed roots and rocks and transforms into a well-maintained path of switchbacks.

There are a couple of small avalanche slopes that open the forest for views, but for the most part this is a journey through an evergreen forest. A little over an hour into the hike will place you at treeline, having

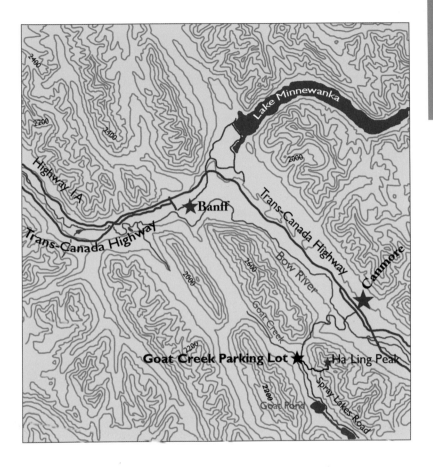

accomplished 292 m of elevation, with 516 m remaining. Another hour of long meandering switchbacks brings the trail to a junction at the col between Ha Ling Peak and Mount Lawrence Grassi. Take the left trail, heading north, and continue along this path up the slope of rock.

Thirty minutes from the col will place you at the summit. The path toward the summit comes precariously close to the south edge of Ha Ling Peak and presents some incredible stomach churning while doing so. There is so much to see from up here. Looking to the northwest is the southeast end of Mount Rundle. Toward the southwest lies the Goat Range, and to the northwest, the Fairholme Range.

History

Ha Ling Peak was named after a Chinese cook, though it is unclear whether he worked for the CPR or a local mine. Either way, in 1896 Ha Ling bet his co-workers $50 that he could summit the peak and return within ten hours. Not only did he accomplish this within the allotted time, he did it in barely half the time and was back by noon for lunch. His co-workers did not witness this accomplishment and with a $50 bet on the line, they did not believe him, either. Luckily, Ha Ling had planted a flag on summit as evidence of his feat, so he led a party to the summit to see the flag and to affix a much larger one in its place that was seen from the town of Canmore. Unofficially named "Chinaman's Peak" at the time, in his "honour," this did not become its official title until 1980. This name did not last long, however, as public pressure got it changed to Ha Ling Peak in 1997. Prior to all of this, the mountain was called "The Beehive."

Mount Lawrence Grassi seen from Ha Ling Peak.

15. GEODETIC SURVEY OF CANADA MARKER 696005 (TWIN PEAKS)

Most rewards in life require tremendous effort to garner a worthy payoff, but sometimes you just simply luck out and discover something extraordinary by accident. This is certainly the case with these prizes, as they were found while searching for something else. Although maybe not quite as monumental as Wilhelm Röntgen's accidental discovery of x-rays in 1895, it still ranks right up there for me. On my second attempt at summiting Mount Cory, I failed once again, but ended up climbing these two lesser peaks instead. These twin summits involve less drudgery and less elevation gain, and with the exception of looking north, they offer the same spectacular scenery that Mount Cory does.

By taking a GPS waypoint atop a Geodetic Survey of Canada marker on the higher of the two peaks, I was able to work with Steve Irwin and Patrice Lascelles of the NRCan in identifying one of the nameless peaks. Actually, Steve and Patrice did all the work, since I simply forwarded the coordinates to them. They have identified the peak as "GSC marker 696005 on the low south tip of Mount Cory in the Sawback Range." Many thanks to Steve and Patrice for their hard work, which produced results for me within a day.

DIFFICULTY ▲ ▲ ▲
ELEVATION GAIN: 964 M

| Trailhead: | GPS: N51 10 08.5 W115 40 54.8 |
| | Elevation: 1414 m |

| Col between summits: | GPS: N51 11 06.0 W115 41 26.0 |
| | Elevation: 2326 m |

| Minor summit: | GPS: N51 11 09.0 W115 41 23.8 |
| | Elevation: 2373 m |

| Main summit: | GPS: N51 11 01.4 W115 41 32.5 |
| | Elevation: 2378 m |

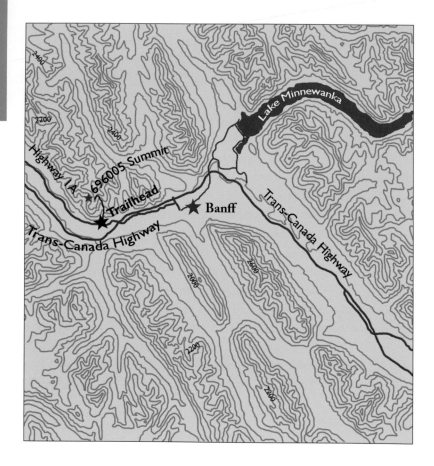

Trailhead: From the west entrance into Banff townsite, travel west for 5.6 km to the Bow Valley Parkway turnoff. At 2 km along this route there is an unmarked turnoff on the right side of the road. This is the trailhead.

Get on the only trail leaving the roadside and follow it straight, crossing under the power lines. Within four to five minutes from the roadside, you will come upon a dried-up, gravel-lined drainage canal. The trail for GSC marker 696005 is well marked on the right, with a cairn, just off the main trail. Be sure that you make this turn and do not carry on up the main trail, as this will take hours off your day and put you at a ridge that ends in a high, steep drop-off (my first unsuccessful attempt at Mount Cory). So, if you have travelled longer than ten minutes, backtrack and look more intently for the intersection.

Once on the trail, you will encounter the most difficult part of the climb within five to ten minutes. In fact, the lateral exposure of the ridge will be in sight within a few moments of turning onto the trail. By taking the best of the many routes available, you can attain the ridge crest within another 10 minutes of moderate scrambling up the side of the ridge. Up on the ridge, cairns and the path come into plain sight.

The only obstacle on the climb is a rock abutment which is reached in about 10 minutes more and is easily circumnavigated by following the track around the bluff into the bushes on the right side. The entire excursion is well marked with cairns and a well-used path, suggesting that either many other scramblers have also lost their way to Mount Cory, or, unlike me, they knew where they were going.

Continue this course until you reach the saddle of the two peaks. As you gaze up at the two peaks, the right one appears to be the highest, but in fact the one on the left (west) is higher by 5 m. The Geological Survey of Canada marker is unmistakable once you've reached the summit. It is a large wooden pyramid filled with rocks straddling the marker, which is firmly secured to the ground in concrete.

Views from this vantage point include Mount Cory directly behind to the north, with the best possible view of the Hole in the Wall. The Hole in the Wall is a dark, yawning cave extending almost 30 m into the southwestern slope of Mount Cory. The Sundance Range is 6.5 km to the southeast (true bearing 156°), and the unmistakable limestone slab of Mount Rundle sits 14.3 km into the horizon almost due east at a true bearing of 100°.

History

The Sawback Range extends south to the Bow River just northwest of the town of Banff, reaching as far north as Bonnet Peak. Other peaks in this range include Mount Cory, Block Mountain, Mount Ishbel, Oyster Peak, Cockscomb Mountain, Mount Louis, Mount Fifi, Mount Edith and The

Finger. The range was named on August 17, 1858, by Sir James Hector (1834–1907), a surgeon and geologist with the Palliser Expedition.

Soon after reaching the Rockies, John Palliser had sent Hector to investigate the geology of the Rocky Mountains. He left present-day Morley, Alberta, on August 11 with the hope of discovering the source of the Bow and a possible pass as a trading route to the Columbia River. Coincidentally, Hector left the same day as Eugène Bourgeau, a botanist with the Palliser Expedition, and the parties travelled together for a day exploring Grotto Mountain. Bourgeau decided to stay near present-day Banff to collect samples of the local plant life, while Hector continued his way over Grotto Mountain to a vast valley where he spent several days collecting fossils, exploring the nearby slopes and allowing time for his party to collect meat for the upcoming adventure.

Finally, on August 17, after spending the previous day arduously exploring Cascade Mountain, Hector set his sights on his objective. Following a map drawn by a Stoney Indian guide Hector named "Nimrod" because he could not pronounce the man's Indian name, the route took them on a long, roundabout track that would eventually bring them to Castle Mountain. The vertical beds of grey limestone that form the serrated peaks of the range present such a jagged appearance that they reminded Hector of a saw, hence the name.

The Sundance Range, looking south from
Geological Survey of Canada Marker 696005.

Opposite: Mount Rundle and Banff town site in
the distance, from Geological Survey of Canada
Marker 696005.

Above: Mount Cory with the Hole-in-the-Wall.
These jagged peaks demonstrate the name,
Sawback Range, bestowed on them by Sir James
Hector in 1858.

183

16. TOWER OF BABEL

The Tower of Babel is an easily accessible scramble with comparatively nominal elevation change, and consequently many scramblers disregard this hike altogether. But do not let this lull you into a false belief that this is somehow a proportionately easy scramble. There is much work involved in attaining this flat summit, even though it is half the height of most of the scrambles in the surrounding area. Although it requires a significant amount of work, the climb can be used for a quick morning or afternoon scramble because of the easy access and small elevation gain.

Mainly a climb of scree through a narrowing gorge, this uncomplicated journey presents no technical challenges. The summit differs from most others in that it is a wide, flat cap plagued with way too many cairns.

DIFFICULTY ▲ ▲ ▲
ELEVATION GAIN: 462 M

Trailhead: GPS: N51 19 42.5 W116 10 30.8
                        Elevation: 1862 m

Tower of Babel Summit: GPS: N51 19 33.0 W116 10 13.9
                        Elevation: 2324 m

Trailhead: From the Lake Louise village, drive up Lake Louise Drive toward the Chateau and turn left on Moraine Lake Road. Continue to the Moraine Lake parking lot, approximately 12 km from the turnoff. Find the trail on the south side of the lot behind the public toilets. Cross the Moraine Lake outlet stream and before long the trail meets its first intersection. Follow the sign to the left to Consolation Lakes over a short avalanche slope. Some boulder hopping is necessary on this rubble.

Looking upward to the right gives the climber a perfect understanding of the commitment that must be made to gain the summit. So, at any time, break to the right into the forest, to arrive at the base of the scree slope to

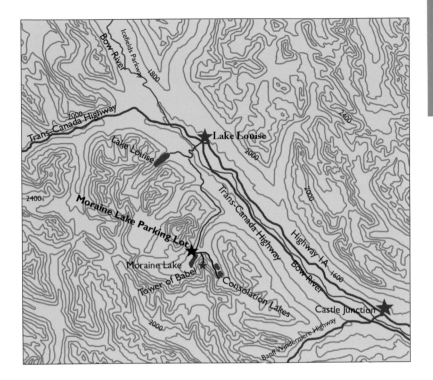

reach the gorge. There are a couple of trails and cairns extending into the forest, but they are difficult to find. Once on the scree slope, begin to climb toward the obvious ravine and look for the main trail ascending along the right side of the scree. The footing is more solid here, and most of the drudgery is substituted with larger rocks and some firm earth. Save the scree slope for a quick descent.

The objective should be evident as the trail progresses upward toward the gaping opening of the ravine. Upon entering this high, steep-walled structure, merge to the right side and clamber up onto a small ridge that parallels the loose scree in the middle. The rock debris in the middle of the gorge is actually more of a soggy, sand-like consistency, making this some of the worst material for climbing. There are minor paths appearing as small game tracks scattered across the little ridge all the way up to the narrowest part of the gorge.

Near the top there is no option but to climb back down to the middle of what now seems more like a canyon and is only a few feet across. The good news is that the scree has all but entirely disappeared. Watch for traffic above you, as there is loose rock and no place to hide from it. A helmet is strongly advised. The path pops out of the narrow gorge to a flat, wide ridge that advances en route to the summit to the left.

The summit is wide, flat and made of limestone slabs, making this one of the most fun summits in the region. There are endless vistas visible from the top, with Panorama Ridge due east, Mount Temple to the northwest and the Consolation valley and lakes to the south.

History

When Walter Wilcox came upon Moraine Lake in 1894 he quite under-standably was under the impression that a large glacial moraine had sealed the lake during the retreat of the Wenkchemna Glacier at the northeast end of the lake. Actually, it was rubble and large boulders fallen from the Tower of Babel and nearby Mount Fay that closed off the lake. As you walk toward the tower, Consolation Lakes or Panorama Ridge, you have to cross this rubble field, and it becomes evident that fallen rocks have formed the natural dam. Even so, there is still a theory and a slim chance that Wilcox may have been correct and that the rock dam could have been deposited by a glacier that reached down from farther up the valley. Wilcox's original vantage point was from the opposite shoreline, so one can understand how anyone could make this honest mistake.

The Tower of Babel had been left unnamed for five years until Wilcox coined the name in 1899. The name is derived from the Tower of Babel mentioned in the Bible in Genesis 11. The story says that a tower "with its top in the heavens" was constructed in the ancient city of Babel (Babylon). After the Flood, the descendants of Noah journeyed to the east and created the city of Babylon along with the Tower.

Walter Wilcox chose an appropriate name, as this unique formation of Gog quartzite indeed appears to reach straight up toward the heavens.

The imposing Tower of Babel from the ascent in the ravine below.

Moraine Lake Lodge from the plateau summit of the Tower of Babel.

Acknowledgements

This book is dedicated to my father, Pat Shea, who always encouraged me to follow my heart, even if I did not know where it was taking me.

I would like to thank my wife, Debbie, for always supporting and encouraging my passion for hiking and scrambling. Also my children, Tyler, Brock and Kelly, who have accompanied me on many of my treks. The excitement in your eyes has always been my driving force.

To my scrambling companions Don Brown, Peter Peller, Tyler Shea, and Nolan Brown, thank you for your patience and laughter.

It is far more enjoyable to share the natural beauty of the mountains with friends and loved ones than to do it alone.

The Journey

Dust arising from the path a new
journey to begin

From the peak to the base, the hills cast
a shadow upon us, as if to grin

Stating their difficulties, we look upon
in awe,
a quest, a trek, a challenge for all

The sweat and the pain; outweighed
by the lush fields, the sweet pure water,
and the rugged terrain

The icy guardians, they lurk up high in
the hills,
watching our every move, grumbling,
they stay still

Pushing through the rain, the snow, and the sleet,
the body is tired.
Your eyes demand more
despite your sore feet

And when the sun comes up, your picture is
perfect, nothing you could have imagined,
and now the journey becomes worth it.

—Tyler Shea

Glossary

bear pole. A pole or cable between two trees, used for hoisting food out of the reach of bears.

cairn. A pile of stones, usually conical in shape, raised as a landmark or a memorial. In prehistoric times, usually erected over a grave. For scrambling and hiking, cairns are used for marking trails.

campground. A designated area for camping, ideally consisting of outhouse(s), bear pole, common cooking/eating area, water source, designated grey-water area, tent pads etc.

campsite. A spot to set up a tent within a campground.

cirque. A steep, bowl-shaped hollow at the upper end of a mountain valley, especially one forming the head of a glacier or stream.

col. A depression in a ridge or range of mountains, generally affording a pass from one slope to another.

grey-water area. A common designated area at a campground where used water can be discarded.

moleskin. A soft material, often with an adhesive backing, used especially on the feet to protect against chafing.

moraine. A buildup of rocks and boulders deposited by a glacier

privy. An outdoor toilet, usually consisting of a pole fastened between two trees for sitting on.

scree. Loose debris consisting of rocks or sand covering the slope of a hill.

Spenco 2nd Skin.™ Moist-wound bandage.

tarn. A small mountain lake formed by glaciers.

Bibliography

Beck, Janice Sanford. *No Ordinary Woman: The Story of Mary Schäffer Warren.* Calgary: Rocky Mountain Books, 2001.

Berry, Oliver, Brendan Sainsbury & Korina Miller. *Banff, Jasper & Glacier National Parks.* Footscray, Vict. (Aust.), Oakland, Calif., and London: Lonely Planet Publications, 2008.

Brink, Nicky L., and Stephen R. Bown. *Forgotten Highways: Wilderness Journeys Down the Historic Trails of the Canadian Rockies.* Edmonton: Brindle & Glass, 2007.

Denny, Sir Cecil E. *Denny's Trek: A Mountie's Memoir of the March West,* 2nd ed. with additions by Rodger Touchie. Surrey, BC: Heritage House, 2004.

Edwards, Ralph. *Trail to the Charmed Land.* Hamilton, Ont.: H.R. Larson, 1950.

Foran, Jill. Mary Schäffer: *An Adventurous Woman's Exploits in the Canadian Rockies.* Amazing Stories series. Canmore, Alta: Altitude Publishing Canada, 2003.

Fraser, Esther. *The Canadian Rockies: Early Travels and Explorations.* Edmonton: Hurtig, 1969.

Hamilton, William B. *The Macmillan Book of Canadian Place Names.* Toronto: Macmillan of Canada, 1983.

Hart, E.J. *Jimmy Simpson, Legend of the Rockies.* Calgary: Rocky Mountain Books, 2009.

Holmgren, Eric J., and Patricia M. Holmgren. *Over 2000 Place Names of Alberta.* Saskatoon: Western Producer Prairie Books, 1977.

Jenish, D'Arcy. *Epic Wanderer David Thompson and the Mapping of the Canadian West.* Lincoln: University of Nebraska Press Bison Books, 2009.

Jenkins, Phil, and George M. Dawson. *Beneath My Feet: The Memoirs of George Mercer Dawson.* Toronto: McClelland & Stewart, 2007.

Karamitsanis, Aphrodite. *Place Names of Alberta.* Calgary: Alberta Culture & Multiculturalism and Friends of Geographical Names of Alberta Society, 1991.

Lakusta, Ernie. *The Intrepid Explorer: James Hector's Explorations in the Canadian Rockies.* Calgary: Fifth House, 2007.

Lothian, William F. *A Brief History of Canada's National Parks.* Ottawa: Minister of Supply & Services Canada, 1987.

Lynx, Dustin. *Hiking Canada's Great Divide Trail,* rev. ed. Calgary: Rocky Mountain Books, 2007.

Many, Kathryn. *Skoki Beyond the Passes: The Story of Western Canada's First Backcountry Ski Lodge.* Calgary: Rocky Mountain Books, 2001.

McCart, Joyce, and Peter J. McCart. *On the Road with David Thompson.* Calgary: Fifth House, 2000.

Nisbet, Jack. *Sources of the River: Tracking David Thompson across Western North America.* Seattle: Sasquatch Books, 2007.

Patton, Brian, ed. *Tales from the Canadian Rockies.* Toronto: McClelland & Stewart, 1993.

Rayburn, Alan. *A Dictionary of Canadian Place Names.* Don Mills, Ont.: Oxford University Press, 2009.

Rayburn, Alan. *Naming Canada: Stories about Canadian Place Names,* rev. ed. Toronto: University of Toronto Press, 2001.

Schäffer Warren, Mary T.S., Mary W.
Adams and Edward J. Hart. *A Hunter
of Peace: Mary T.S. Schäffer's Old Indian
Trails of the Canadian Rockies; Incidents
of Camp and Trail Life, Covering Two
Years' Exploration through the Rocky
Mountains of Canada.* Banff: Whyte
Foundation, 1994.

Scott, Chic. *Powder Pioneers: Ski Stories
from the Canadian Rockies and Columbia
Mountains.* Calgary: Rocky Mountain
Books, 2005.

Simpson, George, and E. E. Rich. *Part of a
Dispatch from G.S., Governor of Rupert's
Land, to the Governor and Committee of
the HBC, London, March 1, 1829. Cont'd
and Completed March 24 and June 5, 1829.*
Toronto and London: The Champlain
Society, 1947.

Spry, Irene M. *The Palliser Expedition: The
Dramatic Story of Western Canadian
Exploration, 1857–1860.* Western
Canadian Classics series. Saskatoon:
Fifth House Publishers, 1995.

Thorington, J. Monroe. *The Glittering
Mountains of Canada: A Record
of Exploration and Pioneer Ascents
in the Canadian Rockies, 1914–1924.*
Philadelphia: J.W. Lea, 1925.

White, James. *Dictionary of Altitudes
in the Dominion of Canada.* Ottawa:
Commission of Conservation Canada,
1916.

Wilson, Thomas Edmund, William E.
Round and Hugh Aylmer Dempsey.
Trail Blazer of the Canadian Rockies.
Calgary: Glenbow-Alberta Institute,
1972.

Yorath, C.J. *How Old Is That Mountain? A
Visitor's Guide to the Geology of Banff and
Yoho National Parks.* Madeira Park, BC:
Harbour Publishing, 2006.

Index of Place Names

193

More Titles from Rocky Mountain Books

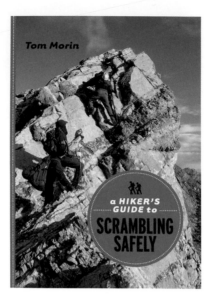

A Hiker's Guide to Scrambling Safely

Tom Morin

Unroped scrambling over so-called easy terrain is one of the most poten-tially dangerous recreational activities. Every year, scramblers are injured or killed in preventable accidents. *A Hiker's Guide to Scrambling Safely* educates new scramblers in the inherent risks and required climbing skills and imparts the mountaineering knowledge necessary for safety when the going gets steep.

ISBN 978-1-894765-66-4

Black & White Photos

$14.95, Softcover

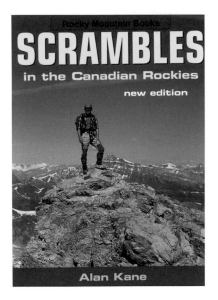

SCRAMBLES

In the Canadian Rockies

Alan Kane

Completely revised and updated with over 50 new scrambles. 156 easy peaks with a wide range of difficulty suitable for novice climbers and experienced hikers who want a little more challenge. Illustrated with 188 route photos.

ISBN 978-0-921102-67-0
Black & White Photos
$29.95, Softcover

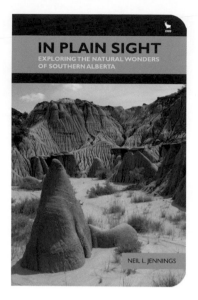

In Plain Sight

Exploring the Natural Wonders of Southern Alberta

Neil L. Jennings

In Plain Sight highlights a selection of natural wonders and outdoor adventures located in southern Alberta. The places featured in this book have been chosen for their utter uniqueness, beauty and splendour. Some are easy to get to and easy to get around in; others require a bit more time and energy. Overall, you will be stimulated, enlightened, delighted, amazed, uplifted and broadened by the experience. These are truly awesome places, in the very real meaning of that word. All are in plain sight, though they are little visited by locals or tourists.

ISBN 978-1-897522-78-3

Colour Photos, Maps

$26.95, Softcover

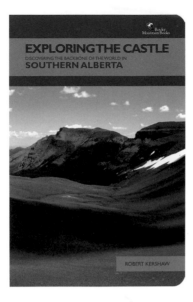

EXPLORING THE CASTLE

Discovering the Backbone of the World in Southern Alberta

Robert Kershaw

In 1901, naturalist George Bird Grinnell took note of an extensive network of mountains, ridges, valleys, lakes and rivers on both sides of the Continental Divide from northern Montana into southern British Columbia and Alberta. Disregarding political boundaries, he named it "The Crown of the Continent." While "Crown of the Continent" speaks eloquently of the region's beauty with more than a passing nod to European monarchy and history, the Blackfoot name carries a more vital and universal meaning: 'Mo'kakiikin,' the 'backbone of the world.' At the heart of this complex landscape lies the Castle Wilderness.

ISBN 978-1-897522-04-2

Colour Photos, Maps

$26.95, Softcover

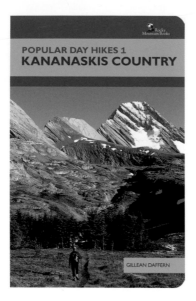

Popular Day Hikes 1
Kananaskis Country

Gillean Daffern

This is a book of popular day hikes in one of southern Alberta's most-loved outdoor recreation areas. Kananaskis Country covers more than 4,000 square hectares of the Canadian Rockies south and east of Banff National Park, and is a favourite destination for outdoors enthusiasts of all ages and abilities. This book features 34 hikes, with detailed descriptions focusing on quality trails with easy access and good staging areas. Factual and informative, *Popular Day Hikes 1* is complete with maps and colour photographs and is sure to satisfy locals and visitors alike.

ISBN 978-1-894765-90-9

Colour Photos, Maps

$15.95, Softcover

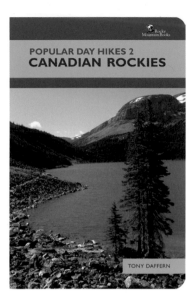

Popular Day Hikes 2
Canadian Rockies

Tony Daffern

Following up on the success of the first book in the Popular Day Hikes series - Gillean Daffern's *Popular Day Hikes 1: Kananaskis Country* - Rocky Mountain Books is thrilled to offer this companion volume focusing on the splendour of the Canadian Rockies. The Popular Day Hikes series is written for visitors and locals looking to hike scenic trails from well-established staging areas. These factual, attractive guides feature detailed maps and colour photographs throughout.

ISBN 978-1-897522-01-1
Colour Photos, Maps
$15.95, Softcover

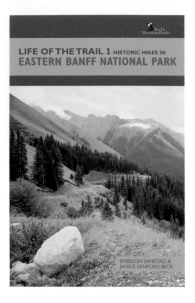

LIFE OF THE TRAIL 1

Historic Hikes in Eastern Banff National Park

Emerson Sanford & Janice Sanford Beck

Life of the Trail 1: Historic Hikes in Eastern Banff National Park follows the trails of David Thompson, Walter Wilcox, the Palliser Expedition, James Carnegie Earl of Southesk, Bill Peyto and A.P. Coleman. Along the way, the reader will journey from the Kootenay Plains to Lake Minnewanka, discovering the stories behind routes through the mountain towns of Banff and Lake Louise and along the Red Deer, Ptarmigan and Skoki valleys.

ISBN 978-1-894765-99-2
Colour and Black & White Photos, Maps
$26.95, Softcover

LIFE OF THE TRAIL 2
Historic Hikes in Northern Yoho National Park

Emerson Sanford & Janice Sanford Beck

Life of the Trail 2: Historic Hikes in Northern Yoho National Park follows the trails of fur traders La Gasse and Le Blanc, the Palliser Expedition, Tom Wilson, J.J. McArthur, Professor Jean Habel, Walter Wilcox, C.S. Thompson, David Thompson, Jimmy Simpson and Jack Brewster. Along the way, the reader will journey past pristine lakes and glaciers that have become legendary throughout the world, discovering the stories behind routes through the mountain towns of Lake Louise and Field; over Howse, Amiskwi, Bow and Burgess passes; and along the Yoho, Emerald and Castleguard rivers.

ISBN 978-1-897522-00-4
Colour and Black & White Photos, Maps
$26.95, Softcover

LIFE OF THE TRAIL 3

The Historic Route from Old Bow Fort to Jasper

Emerson Sanford & Janice Sanford Beck

Life of the Trail 3: The Historic Route from Old Bow Fort to Jasper starts at the remains of Peigan Post, originally built in 1832 and still visible today, located at the west end of the Morley Reserve. This entire route is now a modern road, but in the early 20th century the section north of Lake Louise was the main trail heading north and was very busy with pioneers, adventurers and explorers. The trail has been divided into three sections: Old Bow Fort to Lake Louise, Lake Louise to Sunwapta Pass and Sunwapta Pass to Jasper.

ISBN 978-1-897522-41-7

Colour and Black & White Photos, Maps

$26.95, Softcover

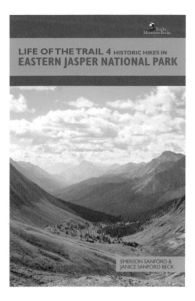

LIFE OF THE TRAIL 4
Historic Hikes in Eastern Jasper National Park

Emerson Sanford & Janice Sanford Beck

Life of the Trail 4: Historic Hikes in Eastern Jasper National Park includes trails throughout the Jasper area, as well as routes in the White Goat Wilderness and part of the Bighorn Wildland, outside the national park. The main trails are fur-trade routes: Duncan McGillivray's along the Brazeau river and Poboktan Creek, Jacques Cardinal's from Jasper to the North Saskatchewan River along the South Boundary Trail and over Job Pass, and Old Klyne's Trail over Maligne and Cataract passes and along the Cline River to the Kootenay Plains. The fourth is a 20th-century route, the Skyline Trail.

ISBN 978-1-897522-42-2

Colour and Black & White Photos, Maps

$26.95, Softcover

GPS Made Easy

Using Global Positioning Systems in the Outdoors

Lawrence Letham & Alex Letham

"Buy this book before you buy your GPS. It will teach you what questions to ask and what the answers mean…there's no better way to learn the ins and outs of GPS." —*News Tribune*, Tacoma, WA

"If you travel far from the beaten path, or in regions without obvious points of reference, GPS can be a tremendous source of security. Letham's book can explain how to make the most of that global navigation system…it's a one-stop source of information." —*Times Leader*, Wilkes-Barre, PA

ISBN 978-1-897522-05-9

Black & White Photos

$19.95, Softcover